how we felt

DESIGNS + TECHNIQUES FROM CONTEMPORARY FELT ARTISTS

CAROL HUBER CYPHER

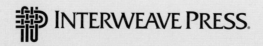
INTERWEAVE PRESS.

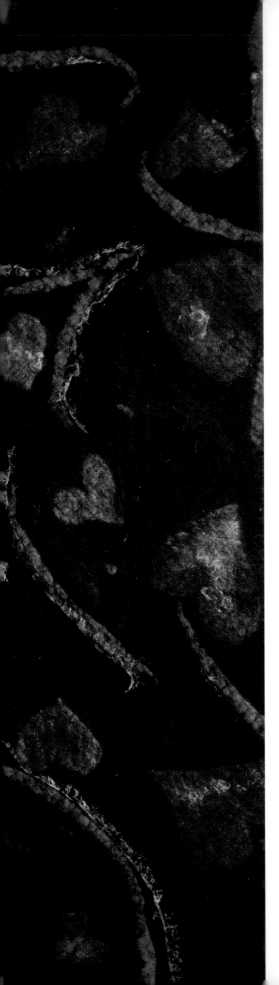

Photography, Joe Coca
Illustrations, Gayle Ford
Cover design, Karla Baker
Interior design, Karen Schober

 Interweave Press LLC
201 East Fourth Street
Loveland, CO 80537-5655 USA
interweavebooks.com

Printed in China by Asia Pacific.

Library of Congress Cataloging-in-Publication Data

Cypher, Carol Huber, 1951-
  How we felt : designs and techniques from contemporary felt artists / Carol Huber
Cypher, author.
    p. cm.
  Includes index.
  ISBN 978-1-59668-031-9 (pbk.)
  1. Felt work. 2. Felting. I. Title.
  TT880.C97 2007
  746'.0463--dc22
                                        2007004752

10 9 8 7 6 5 4 3 2 1

acknowledgments

Jay "Morty" Cypher, my sweetheart, best buddy, voice of reason; Amy Raff, wise friend, librarian super-hero; Susan Vazquez, dear friend and heart of my fiber universe; Phyllis Dintenfass, kindred spirit, cherished friend; Beth Beede, queen mother of an entire generation of feltmakers; and the twenty feltmakers who share how we felt. Thank you.

Barbara Albright was the author of more than two dozen books on food and knitting, including *Knitter's Stash* and *The Natural Knitter*. A few of her books were built around her selection of recipes or designs from fellow foodies and fiber artists. Inspired by the prospect of writing a felt book in that style, I began to compile my list of felters. I'm grateful to have known her and for the memories of her good nature, generous spirit, and infectious laughter.

contents

Introduction

Felt is humble and primal, yet ethereal and beautiful. At once sensuously soft and unyieldingly strong, felt runs the gamut from crude to sublime. Felt is contradiction and contrast. Its production is simple and virtually unchanged over several centuries. Felt is a versatile medium rich in nuances of color and texture and form. The work of making felt, though demanding and considerable, is commonly described as magical and sensuous. Though far from instantaneous, the process enjoys an immediacy that is gratifying and inviting (and often underestimated by the first-timer). Familiar with the degrees and stages of plasticity that wool undergoes between its fluffy-fleece start to its solid-felt finish, the feltmaker "plays" the wool with timing and finesse. Most felt artists acknowledge a partnership with the wool that they describe as an element of kismet that enters the process; finding the muse within the wool; the wool's exerting its will; or a channeled divine or spiritual influence.

Floating Poppies by Linda Brooks Hirschman, page 96

Cocktail Hat by Beth Beede, page 10

Explore the art and elegance of feltmaking in the pages of this book. Embark on an adventure that will inform the way you felt from now on as you step into the studio of each of these accomplished and emerging fiber artists. The artists were asked to use fiber from select readily available sources (see Sources, page 140) and to specify their particular preferences in tools and techniques as they follow the same ten steps from fiber to felt, which are given in Felting Basics (see page 134). Share in their passion and curiosity and benefit by their years of collective experience: best practices, tips, tricks, and variations on the fundamentals of water, agitation, and pressure that have produced felt for thousands of years.

The artists showcased here were chosen for their felt artistry and the expertise, ingenuity, or unique perspective implicit therein. Among their number are professional feltmakers and hobbyists, fiber artists, teachers, and students. Sharing *How We Felt* is meant to inspire and encourage, hone skills, refine techniques, and establish new parameters for felt's potential.

Start by reading Beth Beede's felting around a ball technique. It is the common denominator of many contemporary feltmakers and forms the springboard of many projects in these pages. Building on the fundamentals in Beth Beede's lesson, each successive project shows ways to develop and innovate with a wider array of felting techniques. A gallery of photographs shows additional dramatic, exciting, and artistic pieces to inspire your work in felt and pique your curiosity about the range of felt artists at work today.

Gossamer Saffron Scarf by
Elizabeth Buchtman, page 70

Zabuton Cushion by
Theresa May-O'Brien, page 58

This behind-the-scenes look at the innovations and techniques of contemporary felt art is designed to give the adventurous aspiring feltmaker the tools and confidence to break new ground in her own work. As each of the felt artists in these pages has learned from teachers and peers, let their example inspire how you felt. They wish to thank these teachers: Mary Badcock, Beth Beede, Sharon Costello, Carol Cypher, Sandra Dorn, Chad Alice Hagen, Jean Hicks, May Jacobsen Hvistendahl, and Janette McKeown.

New Dimensions in Felt:
Felting Around a Ball

Felting around a ball produces simple, rounded, three-dimensional felt, which can then be fulled and formed into many shapes. It produces hats of many styles—cloches, berets, small-brimmed hats, pillboxes, caps—as well as masks, bags, vessels, and sculptural forms. This technique, developed by renowned felt artist Beth Beede, offers a successful felt hat-making experience even for first-timers. Her method, a playful and dependable vehicle for teaching a range of feltmaking skills in short order, has spanned several continents and over three decades.

In the following pages, discover the basic skill that almost every felt artist in this book has studied and used as the springboard for unique artistic explorations. After learning the groundwork, explore the possibilities for adding surface designs with mohair locks, shiny glitter, yarn, and silk, or further three-dimensional additions with flaps, ruffles, rolls, pockets, spikes, and cords. As you explore the projects of the most exciting contemporary felt artists, the influence of this simple process to create three-dimensional felt will be abundantly clear.

About the Artist

BETH BEEDE is a world-renowned feltmaker and fiber artist who developed the method of felting around a ball with her husband, Larry, in 1975. Every feltmaker in this book has probably felted around a ball with Beth Beede or with someone who has. Beth taught this technique and an entire repertoire of feltmaking workshops throughout the United States, Canada, Mexico, Hungary, New Zealand, and Australia. Her enthused and enabled students eagerly shared the method with others. Its use grew exponentially over the years, changing and morphing as each felter adapted and altered it. Now retired from teaching, Beth is enjoying the luxury of time—to vacation in Mexico with Larry; to spend with friends or work in the yard, and (she says with enthusiasm) to experiment and work in her studio.

Materials

- 2 oz (60 g) or more (depending on the project) of wool roving or batt

Note: Depending on the thickness and weight of the project, more wool may be needed. Two ounces is optimal for some hats, but a vessel calls for a thicker felt that can be made harder, and a mask takes more wool to develop shapes and form.

In Beth's Studio

- Inflatable plastic ball, 10–12" (25.5–30.5 cm) in diameter

Note: Try a smooth plastic ball from a grocery or drugstore, or an inflatable children's ball from a toy store.

- Basin, tub, or sink large enough to accommodate the ball and both hands
- Cereal bowl
- 3 pairs of pantyhose, each leg knotted close to the seat, with the remaining leg portion cut off (reserve the legs as ties for rolled-up feltmaking)
- Washboard
- Hot soapy water

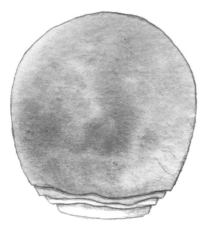

Figure 1. Build 3 perpendicular layers of wool

1. Layer the fiber

Check that the ball is not overinflated; it's important that the ball have a little give when pressed. Steady the ball in the cereal bowl, valve-side down.

After placing surface design, if any, on the ball (see "Surface Decoration, Inside and Out" page 13), build three fairly thin and very even layers of wool over the ball. Place each layer perpendicular to the previous one, down to the edge of the bowl (Figure 1). If your wool is prepared in batt form, lift thin layers from narrow strips; if you are using roving, overlap wisps pulled from the end. Change or layer color anywhere you wish the colors to blend. (The amount of blending depends on the amount of wool and degree of fulling.) When you have placed the three layers of wool, check for thin spots.

Add a design to the surface, if desired. See Surface Decoration on page 14 for options.

2. Place ball within pantyhose

Have a friend help you stretch the top of a pair of pantyhose over the ball, stretching the fabric open and down as you go and being careful not to drag the waistband against the wool. (If you see that the pantyhose won't stretch wide enough, remove the elastic waistband from just this first one.)

Turn the ball upside down and feather the wool—gently tug the fibers to spread them evenly—at the opening, leaving a small hole around the ball plug.

Note: It will be easier to stretch the opening if that area is built with one additional layer of wool or is felted less.

Pull another pair of pantyhose over the ball in the opposite direction from the first pair. Finally, apply the third pair from the side to hold the wool tightly against the ball.

3. Wet and felt

Place the wrapped ball in the basin, tub, or sink, and wet it thoroughly with hot soapy water. Press, push, and roll the ball vigorously against the bottom for one minute. Bounce or dribble it on a table, avoiding hard bounces that would pull the wool apart and off the ball, for two minutes. (Don't expect much bounce from a ball wrapped in wet wool; you are repeatedly dropping the ball onto the table from a short distance.) Remove the outer two pairs of pantyhose. Reveal a bit of the felt and apply the pinch test (see Glossary, page 139). If the fibers are still separate and loose when pinched, put the two pairs of pantyhose back on and continue to work until the fibers do not individually yield to the pinch test.

When the fibers hold together, remove the pantyhose.

4. Remove the ball

For a vessel with a small opening, deflate the ball to remove it. For a hat or bowl, gently stretch the opening until the ball can be eased out and a head could be accommodated.

To allow the ball to be removed, the fibers around the opening are usually stretched to their limit, lining up the individual fibers horizontally. If this causes a rigid edge, cut just a very small amount off of the edge to release the tension.

5. Full (firm and shape felt)

Fulling can be done in many ways: with just your hands, or on a washboard or equivalent textured surface. For most hat styles other than berets, stretch the bottom edge out gently and gather the hat together in the widest area, forming a bell shape. Continue to full the piece by rolling and pressing it against the textured surface. Change the direction of the area being worked by gathering the hat from brim to crown. Alternate between these directions frequently so the felt shrinks evenly.

Note: The wool fibers tangle and shrink in the direction that the felt is pressed, rubbed, or rolled. Control the final size and shape through selective fulling.

Stop fulling when the piece shrinks to about the desired size. Avoid fulling the piece too far, making it too small to stretch over your head or a hat block. If it is still soft and squishy when you have achieved the desired shape and size, rub any soft areas on something like the surface of a glass washboard or piece of ribbed plastic stair tread to continue fulling.

When it is sufficiently fulled, allow the piece to dry or select one of the options for blocking and shaping to a specific form on page 15.

Adapt this flexible technique to other size balls or objects. When knee highs or pantyhose in size 4X cannot accommodate your piece, consider wrapping the work in an ace bandage, the genesis of the felting around a ball technique.

Surface Decoration, Inside and Out

Consider surface design in advance. By placing designs both before and after layering the wool, you can create a reversible piece. If the ball has not acquired a tackiness that develops with use, rub a generous coat of dish detergent on the ball to help the design wool to adhere, then place the design directly on the ball. After building the perpendicular layers of wool for the body of the piece, place a design on top. The surface design placed directly onto the ball is more stable than the outer design, so use this advantage to place the more intricate design first.

Fast drying

To remove most of the water before trying on the piece, roll it in a towel and walk around on the bundle. After you are sure the piece fits, rinse it, dry it in the towel again, and reshape the piece before air-drying.

Surface and Three-dimensional Decoration

Tufts of colored wool, shapes cut from partially felted wool ("prefelts"), pencil roving, unspun silk in different forms, pieces of many fabrics, and yarns are a few items to use for surface design. Add any of the decorative elements described below on top of the base three layers of wool before wrapping the ball with pantyhose. Experiment fearlessly. Ideas that don't pan out can usually be removed.

Surface design
Glitz

Glitz is a very fine synthetic fiber with a metallic coating that is combined with other fibers for use in spinning. It can be locked into the felt by spreading it open in a thin layer and topping it with a very thin veil of wool. (It may not be necessary to veil the glitz if using a very small amount.) Use it sparingly, as too much glitz will behave like a resist.

Yarn

To lock a slick or tightly spun fiber to the surface, cover it with a thin veil of the base color of wool.

Three-dimensional design
Dangling locks and mohair

To keep mohair and wool locks loose except where anchored to the base, separate the clipped end of the hairs, giving each one a chance to become felted. Hold the lock intact, just the way it was clipped off of the animal, and brush the clipped end of the lock with your fingertips to separate them. Then, with dampened fingers, tangle them slightly as though making a spitball. Place this end of the lock where you want to attach it, and cover just that splayed-open and tangled end with a thin layer of the base wool (Figure 1). The rest of the lock is prevented from felting because the wool beneath can't work through the dense, glossy hair. Periodically lift the lock from the surface during fulling.

Prepared cords

Make cords by rolling a "cigar" of wool. Wet all but its "root" end and begin rolling it back and forth along a textured surface (washboard or bubble wrap) until firm and felted. Leave the end to be attached to the felt dry and loose (Figure 2). (If this end gets wet, let it dry.)

There are two options for attaching the felted cords: Either partially felt the surface (see prefelts in Glossary, page 139) and then baste the dry ends to the surface or add the dry root end through the (unknotted) leg holes in the first pantyhose placed over the ball. Then add the other pairs and felt as usual.

Figure 2. Wet and roll the cord to firm, leaving ends dry

Flaps and pockets

Before applying the pantyhose and felting, it is easy to add what will become flaps on the surface of the wool. Make each flap separately by building three even layers of wool. Place a resist (see Felting Basics, page 136) on the wool-covered ball to mark where the flap will be. Allow at least 1" (2.5 cm) of the flap wool to extend beyond the edge of the resist and onto the ball's wool where it is to connect (Figure 3).

Add as many flaps as desired, keeping in mind that you may need to remove the waist elastic on the first pair of pantyhose to accommodate the buildup of wool.

After felting the piece and removing the pantyhose, the flaps can be left as they are or stretched and fulled into ruffles, a tight roll, or other sculptural shapes. A thick flap can produce several spikes by cutting narrow strips at right angles to the surface and rolling each strip between your palms. The cords can be tapered or blunted, or terminated in a ball by tying a knot in the end, winding the knot with wool, saturating them with soapy water and tapping until felting begins, then pressing and rolling into a ball.

Figure 1. Place the splayed-open end and cover with thin base wool

Figure 3. Place three even layers of wool on the resist and 1" (2.5 cm) beyond connecting edge

Figure 4. Extend wool over three edges of a pocket

The process for making a pocket is the same as for a flap, except that the layers of wool extend onto the surface on three of four sides (Figure 4). The resist inside the pocket and extending onto the surface on the fourth side will prevent the inside of the pocket from felting together.

Securing and stabilizing added surface design

To secure these additions, cut and card some very short ends of the same wool (or in some cases even finer, easier to felt wool of the same color). Place a very fine veil between the pieces to be connected. Brush any felted surface that isn't already very soft.

When designing with prefelts or seamlessly joining partially felted pieces, basting stitches stabilize the surfaces to be felted together. Unbasted pieces may slip after they are wet, causing the individual fibers to line up with each other. Parallel fibers slide along each other and are less inclined to knot, tangle, and felt together.

Create Design Features with Shaping and Blocking

With steam and a few tools, the basic shape of felt created around a ball can be stretched and transformed into a variety of shapes. An elegant hat, an artful mask, or a shapely vessel can all be molded using these techniques.

Shaping

Work the areas of hats, masks, bags, or sculpture that will be design features until firm before firming up and shaping the rest. For instance, shape a pillbox hat by repeatedly pinching the creased edge between the side and top surfaces until it is firm. Ignore the strange shape of the rest. Only after that crease is firm should you firm up and full the sides and top by rubbing it on a fulling surface. If the sides appear to curve in a little below the top edge, just stretch the piece sideways only in that area until the sides are straight up and down. Just about any shape can be made in this way.

Blocking

Styling with various shaped hat blocks is easy and fun; it works particularly well with "puzzle" blocks (adjustable wooden hat blocks). Achieve professional results with a little effort: Place the felt piece, fulled until slightly smaller than the block, over a continuously steaming electric tea kettle or other steam source until the fabric is very hot. Pull the felt over the form. Immediately begin rolling it with a piece of dowel or rubbing it with smooth objects until the hat is very firm and smooth and fits the form exactly. More steam can be added with an iron and damp cloth or professional steamer as you work it on the block. If possible, let it cool and dry on the block before removing, to maintain size and shape.

projects

Autumn Winds Vessel

About the Artist

SHARON COSTELLO has been a felt-maker for twenty-two years and has made it her full-time profession for the last twelve. Known for her needle-felted art dolls and vessels, she has been featured in several magazines, newsletters, and shows from New York to California. She studied in the United States, Turkey, and Scandinavia, and she teaches in the United States, Canada, and the United Kingdom. Her feltmaking business, Black Sheep Designs, offers supplies, books, and her own videos. Sharon holds a BID (bachelor of industrial design) from Syracuse University and an MBA from the State University of New York at Albany.

Sharon Costello finds the vessel a compelling sculptural form. She is drawn to its feminine symbolism: women as vessels of life, love, and cultural traditions, and women as the keepers of sacred and everyday rituals. Sharon's vessels are inspired by elements of nature: water, wind, earth, and air. This vessel evokes autumn in the Northeast, with colors that progress from greens to reds and golds. A veil of richly dyed silk imparts a misty finish and subtle luster. Colorful layers of wool convey the movement of swirling leaves with strategically placed incisions into the surface. Sharon captures the glint of sunlight off raindrops with the judicious use of bead embroidery.

Though a textile, felt can be made three-dimensional seamlessly and without the use of stabilizers and armature.

Key Techniques

- *Create surface design before felting with silk caps*
- *Layer colored wool for surface color variation*
- *Add surface decoration mid-felting*
- *Sculpt and shape while fulling*
- *Embellish with stitches and beads*
- *Carve after felting*

Materials

- At least 4 contrasting colors of merino wool batt, 6 oz (180 g) total
- Multicolored dyed silk cap
- 15" (38 cm) slubby or thick and thin wool yarn
- Beading thread
- 2 g assorted seed beads

In Sharon's Studio

- Inflatable ball, 10–12" (25.5–30.5 cm)
- 7" (18 cm) plastic flowerpot or large cereal bowl
- Plastic dishpan, 14" (35.5 cm) across
- 3 pairs pantyhose, extra-large (not control top)
- Plain liquid dishwashing soap (no additives)
- 38-gauge felting needle
- Foam sponge or piece of upholstery foam
- Washboard, rubber welcome mat, or other fulling surface
- Small square of ridged stair tread
- Steamer or kettle
- Mixing spoons and shoe horn (to shape while stretching)
- 16–18" (40.5–45.5 cm) long piece of 3" or 4" PVC pipe
- Small Fiskars spring-loaded sharp-pointed scissors
- Beading needle

Finished measurements

10" (25.5 cm) tall; 8" (20.5 cm) wide; 7" (18 cm) deep, 2" (5 cm) base, 2" (5 cm) opening.

Create surface design with silk caps

Before making the basic vessel using Beth Beede's method of felting around a ball, Sharon unfolds the silk cap and pinches the surface to raise a few fibers. Lifting these fibers separates an entire layer of silk web from the rest.

Sharon steadies the ball on top of the flowerpot, then drapes 2 or 3 thin layers of silk over the ball's surface (Figure 1); if too many layers are used, wool cannot migrate through them, and they will not be secure.

Keep in mind when considering surface design that this vessel is not only created from the inside out, it is also created upside down. This first layer placed on the ball becomes the vessel's outermost layer. (Additional surface decoration can be added later in the felting process.)

Layer colored wool

Working from the top down, Sharon covers the entire ball above the flowerpot with 4 thin, even layers of wool (Figure 2), some composed of patches of more than one color.

She changes colors in each layer, alternating contrasting colors (those opposite each other on the color wheel) for optimal effect when carved. She also varies the value (lightness and darkness) of the layers, keeping in mind that light colors may wash out the richness of dark colors. Some fibers migrate into adjacent layers, producing a heathery effect.

When making a vessel with a small or narrow opening like this one, Sharon avoids thick layers of wool at the bottom of the ball (which will be the top of the vessel). She makes every other layer a little short in that area to minimize the thickness of the wool.

She uses vertical strips of wool for the final layer, as they are more likely to remain in place when the pantyhose are applied. If only short pieces remain, she layers them like shingles with the edges slightly overlapped and presses them into the ball.

Silk caps, hankies, and mawatas

The highest quality silk is unraveled in a continuous strand from an intact cocoon. Cocoons punctured by the exiting silk moth, no longer intact, are degummed and spread into layers. Stacked layers (*mawatas*) are labeled as caps, bells, hankies, or squares, reflecting the shape of the frame or form used to make them. To use, open them up and separate the layers.

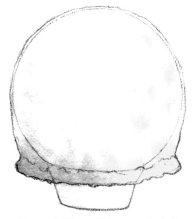

Figure 1. Place silk caps on the ball

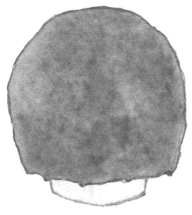

Figure 2. Place four layers of colored wool on the ball over the silk

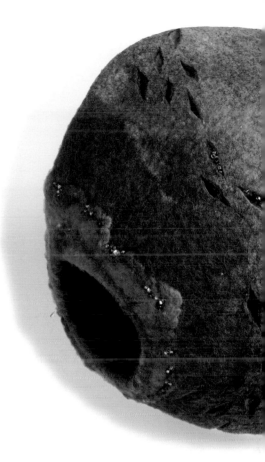

Wrap and felt

Once she is satisfied with the placement of the 4 layers, Sharon wraps the ball with 3 pairs of pantyhose, then wets and felts the wool as in Beth Beede's technique. To avoid dislodging the silk cap, she never bounces the ball, but turns and presses it inside the plastic dishpan until felted. She drains out most excess water from the pan as soon as the wool is wet and pressed tightly around the ball. Working in water or bouncing the ball may cause the wool to shift and dislodge the silk cap and other surface design. This gentler approach adds about 10 minutes to the felting process, until the wool begins to work through the pantyhose and passes the pinch test (see Glossary, page 139). When the wool is felted, she removes the ball.

Second chance to add surface design

Once the wool has felted, Sharon deflates the ball and carefully turns the felt right-side out, taking this opportunity to add slubby yarn to the top. She dries the vessel, then uses a felt needle to place the yarn surface decoration near the top.

When its appearance is satisfactory, she reinflates the ball within the vessel, reapplies the pantyhose, and saturates the vessel with hot soapy water before resuming fulling.

Sculpt and shape while fulling

Sharon keeps the vessel inside out for most of the fulling to protect the surface design. After removing the deflated ball, she rewets the vessel with hot soapy water and, working gently at first, rolls it on the washboard in the direction she wants it to shrink. (For a tall and narrow vessel, she rolls it across its width; for a short bowl, she rolls across its length.) As the vessel shrinks, she applies more pressure, as though kneading bread. Producing this shape requires more rolling of the bottom third. She also uses her fist to stretch the vessel to increase its height while fulling.

Increasing pressure on the felt and reheating the piece in hot water produces dramatic results, and Sharon pays close attention so as not to shrink the piece too much.

The piece hardens as it fulls. Because this vessel will be cut to reveal underlying layers, it must be very hard all the way through.

Shape the rim

To smooth a ragged rim of the vessel, Sharon trims it before she finishes fulling so the cut edge will "heal." To accentuate an uneven edge, she pulls up on certain areas while steaming the vessel.

For a rolled rim, Sharon places one hand inside and one outside the vessel. She rolls the edge back and forth between her hands along the sides of the vessel, working around a little at a time. To narrow the opening, gather it and roll across its width on the fulling surface.

Figure 3. Stretch and pinch a base on the bottom

Shape the base

When the vessel is firm, a third smaller than its original size, and roughly the desired shape, Sharon rinses out the soap, towel-dries the vessel, and turns it right-side out to create a base similar to that of a wine bottle.

She steams the inside of the vessel over a boiling kettle, then pulls the vessel down hard over the PVC pipe, centering the bottom on the pipe. She repeats this process of softening with steam and pulling and stretching over the pipe until the vessel is 10" (25.5 cm) high (Figure 3). Then she alternates between steaming and pinching the vessel's bottom around the rim of the pipe. Done repeatedly, this makes the felt stiff and gives it a "memory" for this shape.

Shape the sides

Once the base is defined, she stretches the sides of the vessel by pressing spoons, shoe horns, or other blunt objects against it from the inside while rubbing the outside surface with a piece of plastic stair tread. The midsection is worked several times in this manner to achieve the desired shape.

The widest part of this vessel's circumference is one-third of the way from the top. Wider than it is deep, the vessel is somewhat flattened.

Place surface design after fulling

When the basic form of the vessel is complete and after the vessel has dried, Sharon uses several techniques to embellish the surface, both adding to and subtracting from the basic vessel. She shaves the fuzzy areas with a razor to increase the sheen of the silk.

Stitch embellishment

Sharon stitches to create surface design, either by hand or with a sewing machine. Her designs take into account the difficulty of stitching the bottom third and the relative ease of sewing horizontal lines rather than vertical ones. (An accomplished machine stitcher with access to a "free arm" attachment could create similar effects without handsewing.)

Carve the surface

Sharon uses very sharp small scissors to make small cuts one at a time, allowing a group of cuts (rather than one large cut) to define a pattern. Her cuts vary in depth to expose different layers of color. This vessel was cut down through 2 multicolored layers to reveal the third one, in a pattern of swirling leaves.

Bead embellishment

Seed beads sewn inside selected cuts draw the eye to that area and add light to the surface. Sharon attaches them with a beading needle and thread. After anchoring the thread in the felt using half hitch knots, she brings the needle up inside a cutout. She strings 3, 5, or 7 beads, allowing them to settle on the surface. She passes back into the felt, working the thread through the felt to emerge from another cutout. She also attaches a few beads along the slubby yarn at the rim.

Think twice, cut once

- Start with a small nip using precision scissors, like spring-loaded Fiskars. A hole can always be made bigger, but never smaller.
- Don't make the mistake of making too few cuts—make sure you have enough cuts to make a statement, creating dramatic motion, pattern and texture on the surface.
- Stressed at the thought of cutting? Make a small flat felted sample to practice on.

Crown of Autumn Leaves

About the Artist
OMI GRAY conducts workshops in silver metal clay and beadwork in her studio in Harlem, New York, and her family-operated hair salon in White Plains, New York. Her creative journey includes metal, silver metal clay, beadwork, fabric dyeing, and painting. Felt offers a soft complement to her metal work.

Omi Gray comes from a long line of hairstylists. Her earliest work with fiber was hairstyling in the tradition of Madame C.J. Walker, using a range of techniques from age-old African to new and innovative.

Her affinity for feltmaking was apparent from the first time she was introduced to it. Parallels between feltmaking and her experience working with hair might explain Omi's penchant for creating hats or, as she calls them, crowns of glory. Enjoying the painterly aspect of working with colored wool, Omi evokes the flight of falling leaves with tapered wisps of roving. By experimenting freely with Beth Beede's method and substituting other forms for the ball, she has developed interesting and exaggerated shapes and sizes. Finding that her preconceived notions seldom matched the outcomes, she has decided that each hat is a shared product of her intentions, trial and error, divine inspiration, and creativity.

Key Techniques
- *Felt around something other than a ball*
- *Create watercolor effects in wool*
- *Wrap piece with mosquito netting*

Materials

- 3½ oz (105 g) solid-colored merino in main color
- ½ oz (14 g) solid-colored merino, divided among 8 accent colors

In Omi's Studio

- Metal mesh wastebasket, 14½" (37 cm) tall, 11½" (29 cm) top radius, 9½" (24 cm) bottom radius
- Bubble wrap, at least 48 × 14" (122 × 38.5 cm)
- Scissors
- Packing tape
- Permanent marker
- Mosquito mesh fabric
- Stretchy lace bodysuit
- Basin
- Olive oil soap
- Sponge
- Towels
- Steam iron
- Spray bottle
- 9" (23 cm) tall vase, 23" (58.5 cm) or less in diameter
- Textured rubber bath mat
- 2 oz vinegar

Finished measurements

9" (23 cm) tall; 23" (58.5 cm) circumference; 2" (5 cm) brim; 35" (89 cm) brim circumference.

Prepare the wastebasket

When felting around a form other than a ball, Omi wraps it with bubble wrap, bubble-side out. One attribute of felting around a ball is the ball's responsiveness to the feltmaker's pressing and rolling. Bubble wrap extends that same yielding property to flat felting.

To cover this wastebasket, she cuts a rectangle of bubble wrap 14½ x 35½" (37 x 90 cm) and wraps it around the basket, marking where the ends meet. Trimming along the marks, she rewraps the basket and tapes the seam. She traces the outline of the basket's bottom on the remaining 12" (30.5 cm) of bubble wrap, cuts along the outline, and tapes this circle to the bottom of the basket. She turns the basket upside down onto a towel-covered table.

Surface design: Wool as watercolor

Omi wraps 4 perpendicular layers of roving on the covered basket (Figure 1). On top of the fourth layer, Omi "paints" the falling leaves design with wisps of colorful roving. She divides the roving lengthwise to achieve the desired width of the "brushstroke." She pinches the tip of this narrow roving and pulls off a wisp of fiber. Layering these, she achieves the effect of brush strokes. For the leafy look, she tapers the wisps at both ends. Their diagonal placement hints at movement.

Cover the basket and wool

Omi replaces the usual pantyhose with a stretchy lace bodysuit, which is larger and easier to handle, when working with pieces of this size. Before wrestling the woolly mass into the bodysuit, she protects the decorated surface with mosquito netting (Figure 2).

Felters accustomed to working solo experiment with alternatives to or easier methods of applying pantyhose. Large pieces of netting draped over the piece and gathered at the bottom result in pleats and folds that become flaps during felting. Winding strips of netting around the piece, bandage-like, offers more control and secures the wool before applying pantyhose or in this case a stretchy bodysuit.

Figure 1. Wrap the covered basket with four perpendicular layers of wool

Figure 2. Wrap wool and basket with mosquito netting

Wet and felt

Omi uses a sponge to saturate the wool with hot soapy water by pressing it into the bodysuit repeatedly. The wool is in less jeopardy of slumping and pooling than if dunked.

She rubs and massages the surface, occasionally with a piece of bubble wrap, until felted.

Shape and full

When the hat passes the pinch test (see Glossary, page 139), Omi removes it from the basket and commences fulling. To accelerate the process, she dunks the hat in hot water and throws it repeatedly onto the textured rubber bath mat.

At this point, she begins to shape the brim and add pleats. Turning up 2" (5 cm) of the brim, she rolls it back and forth, pressing the brim up onto the hat (Figure 3). This stiffens and firms it. She places the hat on the vase, then pinches a pleat nearly 1" (2.5 cm) tall, extending 3" (7.5 cm) from the top center (Figure 4).

She firms the pleats by rolling each between her fingers. For the hat shown here, she made 5 evenly spaced pleats radiating from the center of the top of the hat.

If repeatedly steamed with an iron and then rolled and pinched, the pleats will hold their shape. She pins the pleats in place when she props the hat on the vase to dry, so the weight of the wet hat doesn't distort them.

Figure 3. Press the brim back

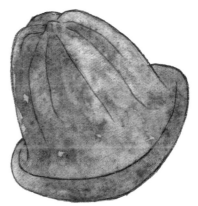

Figure 4. Pinch pleats in the crown

Magnolia Lariat

About the Artist

GAIL CROSMAN MOORE'S bead-work has been published in *Beadwork*, *Lapidary Journal*, and *Bead and Button* magazines. Formerly an art teacher, she applied for a "renewal for teachers" grant to study feltmaking. Once awarded the grant, she purchased books, supplies, and fleece, and took up felting. She became a full-time artist four years ago. Gail exhibits her beads, finished jewelry, and beaded felt compositions at bead shows and conferences.

Gail Crosman Moore has been making glass beads for over a decade. Wanting to make a material to juxtapose against her glass beads, she decided to pursue feltmaking.

Gail's feltmaking began with pods, seeds, and eggs, the same "kernels of the life force" that inform much of her lampworked glass. Capable of volume, felt is ideal for rendering these shapes. She embellishes these intriguing forms with beads.

Her floral pieces suggest what might happen if one of her glass or felt seedpods were to open or hatch. She controls the form they will assume as well as the textures, color, and interaction of light on the surfaces that are at once matte and shiny, soft and hard, felt and glass.

Key Techniques

- *Felt a rope*
- *Felt around an egg shape*
- *Build additional felt mass on the end of the rope*
- *Cut and embellish components*
- *Assemble a lariat*
- *Integrate focal beads*

Materials

- ¾ oz (24 g) merino batt in flower color for flower and pod/bud
- ¾ oz (24 g) merino roving in green for rope
- ¾ oz (24 g) merino roving in green for leaves and calyx
- 15 dozen clear rainbow-finish sequins
- 1 g each of sizes 14°, 11°, 8°, and 6° seed beads
- 1 g Japanese drop beads
- 1 focal bead
- Beading thread

In Gail's Studio

- 2" (5 cm) egg-shaped armature, such as a hollow plastic ornament or solid cedar sachet
- Ribbed surface such as boot mat or shelf lining
- Sushi mat
- Bubble wrap, napkin to placemat size
- Shoebox-size plastic container
- Ivory soap
- Scissors
- Beading needle, size 10 or 12
- Towels
- Empty bottle, such as a plastic dish detergent or shampoo bottle

Finished measurements

Stem: 43" (109 cm) long.
Leaf: 4½ × 4½" (11.5 × 11.5 cm).
Flower: 2½ × 2½ × 2½" (6.5 × 6.5 × 6.5 cm).
Bud or pod: 5½ × 1¼ × 1¼" (14 × 3.2 × 3.2 cm).

Make rope stem

Gail crosses a patch of vertically placed side-by-side wisps of roving with a piece of roving in the length desired for the rope (Figure 1). Twisting the wool approximates the finished diameter of the rope; she splits the roving lengthwise for thinner ropes. She rolls the roving forward to collect the wisps.

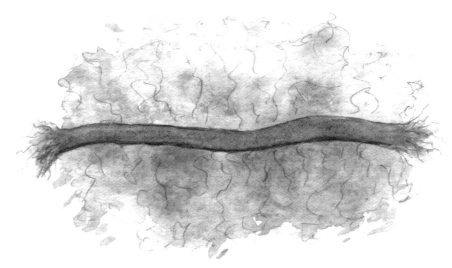

Figure 1. Place a length of roving across wisps of roving

Working on the ribbed surface sprinkled with hot soapy water, she rolls the rope back and forth very gently, as though "handling a newborn baby." She works the entire length a few inches at a time until a skin forms on the soft roll. Sometimes she continues rolling within the folded sushi mat, which applies pressure evenly over a broad surface (Figure 2). When it passes the pinch test (see Glossary, page 139), she applies increasing pressure, fulling it. She scrunches the entire piece and rubs it vigorously between her hands. She kneads and presses it into the ribbed surface. She throws it hard into the sink, working until it is solid.

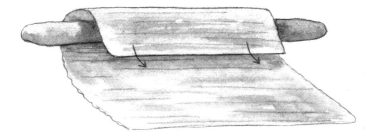

Figure 2. Roll the rope back and forth within sushi mat until solid

Figure 3. Wrap the knot in wool

*Figure 4. Wrap the egg shape
with crossed strips of wool*

Thick and even fiber

To determine that she has laid the wool out evenly, Gail closes her eyes while patting the surface, feeling for thin or heavy spots. The thickness of the layers determines the density of the finished felt. It is common to underestimate the amount of wool necessary. Though a covering of fiber appears thick and lofty when dry, the same amount of fiber may yield a tissue-thin felt.

Shape bud or pod

Gail ties a knot at one end of the rope. Using long, narrow strips of batt, she wraps the knot as though bandaging it in gauze (Figure 3).

She dunks the knot into the plastic shoebox filled with hot soapy water, firmly supported in her hands, to saturate it. She rubs and rolls it gently to form a skin, applying more pressure as it firms, felting and then fulling while tapering the end. She curves the tip after rinsing, allowing it to dry in this position.

Shape flower petals

Using 1½" (3.8 cm) wide strips of consistently dense wool pulled from the batt, she wraps the egg shape in a small-scale version of felting around a ball. She covers three-fourths of the egg, avoiding the narrow end (Figure 4).

Gail cups the fleece-covered egg in her palms and submerges it into the plastic shoebox of hot soapy water. When the air bubbles have ceased and the wool is saturated, she removes it from the bath while supporting the wet, loose fibers. Cradling the egg in one hand, she pats the egg's surface with a liberally soaped other hand to promote formation of the felt's "skin." When the skin is formed, she felts the piece by adding pressure and vigorously rolling the egg over the ribbed mat.

Once the flower cup is felted, Gail removes the egg from the felt. If it doesn't slip out, she snips the narrow end. For the lariat shown here, Gail made another flower cup slightly smaller than the first. She also made a longer, thinner cup for the bud's calyx using 6" (15 cm) of green roving, working it more widthwise than lengthwise.

Make flat felt for leaves

Gail makes flat felt yardage from which to cut several leaves. A square foot of felt made of 2 oz (60 g) of merino wool is more than sufficient for this lariat. She wet-felts 3 perpendicular layers of wool laid out in a 18" (45.5 cm) square (see Glossary, page 134).

Cut and embellish the components

Gail creates an inventory of cups, ropes, and flat pieces. She cuts and embellishes these components with stitches and beads, then assembles them into lariats.

Cut and bead cups to form flowers

To create petals, Gail cuts 3 equally spaced longitudinal lines on the cups, stopping ¾"
(2 cm) from the center (Figure 5). With the beading needle and thread, she dots the
outer surface of the larger flower with sequins, each one held in place with a small size
14° or 11° clear seed bead used as a turning bead (Figure 6).

Cut and bead cup to form calyx

The green cup is also trisected but cut only midway. The base of the calyx is dotted
with green size 11° seed beads.

Cut, stitch, and bead leaf

Gail makes paper templates of leaves to trace and cut out of the flat felt. She animates
each leaf by sewing a midline rib down its length to decorate with a line of side-by-side
size 6° seed beads, each secured with a size 14° seed bead as a turning bead. Gail
dots half of the top side of the leaf with size 6° and the other half with size 8° seed
beads, using size 14° seed beads for turning beads (Figure 7).

Assemble lariat

Gail punctures a hole in the center of each cup. She pulls the unknotted end of the
rope through the inside of the calyx cup, settling the bud into place, before pulling it
through the larger and then smaller flower cups.

   She snugs up the cups, then secures and embellishes at the same time by dotting
the stem at that point with size 14° seed beads. She sews the base of the leaf to the
stem 5" (12.5 cm) from the flower with small invisible stitches.

Create focal bead flower center

She strings the handmade bead onto the rope stem, folding over the last ¾" (2 cm),
and stitches the folded rope into place (Figure 8).

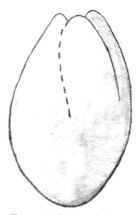

*Figure 5. Cut petals from
egg-shaped cups*

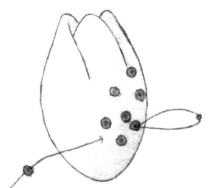

*Figure 6. Dot the surface with
sequins and clear turning beads*

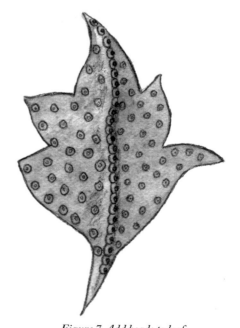

Figure 7. Add beads to leaf

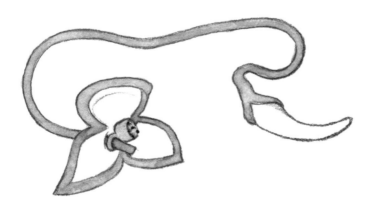

Figure 8. Sew focal bead to flower center

The Brick House Handbag

About the Artist
LISA KLAKULAK received a BFA in fiber art from Colorado State University in 1997 but didn't happen into feltmaking until 2002. At the Penland School of Crafts she learned how to felt around a form and make flat felt with bubble wrap. The three-year intensive residency that followed at the Appalachian Center for Craft allowed her to concentrate on and explore her new medium; during this period she also took a hatmaking workshop. Lisa's wearable art and sculpture are available through select shows and galleries. She teaches natural dyeing and felting workshops.

Lisa Klakulak cites our need to protect our vulnerable human selves as the inspiration for her handbag series. Handbags carry and secure our basic necessities: money, identification, license, photos, keys, and personal treasured items. Lisa's handbags serve as a metaphor for home, the safe haven to us and our possessions. The nursery rhyme of the Three Little Pigs tells us the safest house is made of brick. This handbag's shingle texture and brick patterning is evocative of that house, the ultimate protection. Lisa uses shellac as a stiffening agent, creating a bag that combines softness with rigidity.

Key Techniques

- *Create and incorporate prefelt*
- *Design with prefelts, resists, and stitches*
- *Add tubing armature to handles*
- *Use a magnetic closure*
- *Apply shellac as stiffening medium*

Materials

- 6½ oz (195 g) merino batt, one half for bag, one half for design
- 35" (89 cm) translucent poly tubing, ⅜" (1 cm) diameter
- 4 rare earth magnets
- ½ cup (120 ml) blond shellac flakes
- 3 cups (720 ml) denatured alcohol
- Mercerized cotton sewing thread
- 3-ply waxed linen

In Lisa's studio

- 12" (30.5 cm) inflatable ball
- 2 pieces of bubble wrap with small bubbles, 12 × 40" (30.5 × 101.5 cm) each
- 12 × 40" (30.5 × 101.5 cm) sheet of plastic
- 12" (30.5 cm) PVC pipe, 1" (2.5 cm) in diameter
- Plastic shopping bag
- 4 rubber bands
- Measuring tape
- Scissors
- Rotary cutter and mat
- Lemon Joy liquid soap
- 16 oz (480 ml) spray bottle
- 2" (5 cm) sewing needle
- Pliers (optional, to pull the needle through tough areas)
- 1 pair large-size pantyhose
- Basin, tub, or sink large enough to accommodate the ball and mat
- Doormat with parallel ridges that reverses to ¼" (6mm) stubble texture
- Steamer or kettle
- Towels
- Cereal bowl
- Ziplock bags
- 1 qt (960 ml) Mason jar
- Natural bristle brush
- Tight-fitting latex gloves
- Wire brush, barbecue or suede shoe type
- Pins

Finished measurements

9½" (24 cm) tall; 9½" (24 cm) wide; 4½" (11.5 cm) deep.

Create prefelts

Before making the basic bag shape by felting around a ball, Lisa prepares partially felted fabric for the surface decoration called "prefelts." She spreads out a sheet of bubble wrap, bubble-side down, then places a second piece on top of it, bubble-side up.

She divides one ounce (30 g) of batt into several thin sheets. She then covers a 10 x 18" (21.5 x 45.5 cm) area of the bubble wrap surface with a sheet (or strips pulled from a sheet), crosses this with another layer perpendicular to the first, and repeats until she has placed 3 to 5 perpendicular layers. To assure consistent thickness, she overlaps the layers to the edge and tucks the edges under to keep them thick and blunt.

After filling the spray bottle with hot water and ½ teaspoon (2.5 ml) dishwashing liquid, Lisa sprays the wool until it is saturated. She covers the wet wool with the sheet of plastic in preparation for rolling it until partially felted.

Lisa slides the bottom layer of bubble wrap out 3" (7.5 cm) and places the PVC pipe on this single flat layer. She rolls it up tightly with even pressure and secures both ends with rubber bands. To retain the heat and contain the water, Lisa places the roll in a plastic bag.

Rolling gently with her forearms from fingertips to elbow, applying no pressure, Lisa works for a few minutes, then unrolls and pinch-tests. She rerolls from another edge and resumes working for a few more minutes before applying the pinch test again to monitor progress. When some fibers resist the pinch, she stops. She rinses the prefelt and allows it to dry.

For the bag shown here, Lisa made 3 prefelts: brown, black, and red.

Mix shellac solution

To stiffen the purse, Lisa uses a shellac solution, which requires several days of lead time.

Lisa mixes ½ cup (120 ml) of blond shellac flakes into 3 cups (720 ml) of denatured alcohol in the Mason jar. She performs this step outdoors, as denatured alcohol is extremely flammable and stinky. It takes more than a day for the flakes to dissolve into solution.

Cover the ball with wool

Lisa gently tears the 3½ oz (45 g) of wool batt into 40 x 10" (101.5 x 25.5 cm) strips, from which she lifts thin sheets of fiber. She wraps the inflated ball in these strips of wool until it is uniformly and thoroughly covered. She places another layer of wool around the ball cross-hatching the first layer. She repeats until she has used all the fiber and produced 5 layers. She puts the wool covered ball aside while preparing the prefelt designs.

Cut prefelts for surface design

Although scissors work well to cut designs from the prefelt, Lisa found cutting the rectangles for the design of this bag a breeze when she used a rotary cutter. She cut 44 1 x 1.5" (1.5 x 3.8 cm) "bricks" from the red prefelt, 52 ¾ x 1" (2 x 2.5 cm) "shingles" from the black prefelt, and an 8 x 13" (20.5 x 33 cm) patch from the remaining brown piece.

Attach the prefelt designs to the background

It is necessary to baste prefelt pieces to secure them for felting. Being careful not to stab the ball, Lisa whipstitches the edge of the prefelt designs to the fleece, making stitches that are both functional and decorative (Figure 1). Lisa chooses thread for its texture and detail as additional surface design, allowing them to remain and become part of the surface. Some pieces are stitched down completely. Others are flaps that Lisa makes by stitching one edge of the prefelt piece and using a resist made by cutting strips from a ziplock bag. She stitches a piece of the plastic to the fleece where the prefelt design is to resist becoming felted into the surface. The stitched edge of the prefelt design extends beyond the plastic to fell into the bag, creating a flap like the shingles on this bag.

Lisa places the prepared ball in a pair of pantyhose. *Caution:* Do not cover the prefelt designs with base fleece, disrupt the design, or cause creases and wrinkles.

Felt the bag

Lisa pays particular attention to prefelt areas while felting around the ball, compressing and rubbing them carefully to help them attach to the base. She is particularly cautious of these areas while removing the pantyhose when the felt is firm, and the prefelts are securely felted into the base.

Figure 1. Whipstitch prefelts in place

Back-to-back bubble wrap

Bubble wrap or its hearty "industrial strength" version, solar pool/spa cover, is ubiquitous in rolling felt. Some feltmakers employ it bubble-side up, others bubble-side down. Lisa does both at once! She likes the intensity provided by surrounding the wool with bubbles from above and below. To get this effect, a felter might be tempted to place the wool on the bubble-side-up piece and then cover it with a sheet laid bubble-side down. Lisa cautions that rolling this sandwich shifts the fibers too much, making for uneven and even holey felt. Lisa's back-to-back method achieves the desired effect without those hazards.

Felting solo

It is a bit pesky to slip the pantyhose over a wool-covered ball without a pair of helping hands. Lisa suggests that solitary feltmakers employ the assistance of a wide-mouth bucket or container. Cut off the elastic waistband from the top of the pantyhose. Stretch them over a bucket wider than the ball. Place the ball into the pantyhose top first so that any flap designs are not lifted back. As you gently push the ball down, allow the nylon to slip up the edge of the bucket, falling in and around the ball. Tie the opposite sides of the nylon together in 2 knots.

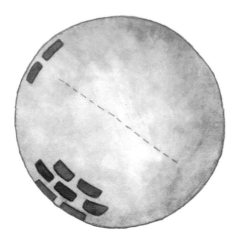

*Figure 2. Cut the felt to produce
the edge of the handles*

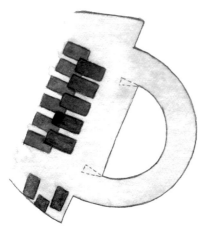

Figure 3. Cut handles and flaps to cover magnets

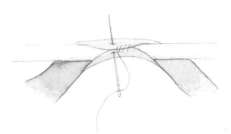

Figure 4. Sew tubing into handles

Cut the bag and remove the ball

She cuts into the felt above the shingles (surface design flaps) both to remove the ball and to prepare for the handles. Lisa inscribes a line with the scissors' edge before cutting an 11" (28 cm) line, which will become the top edge of both handles (Figure 2). After removing the ball through this slit in the felt, she proceeds to full the bag by kneading it along the doormat.

Create self-handles with vinyl tubing armature

This bag uses self-handles, trimmed portions of the bag that will encase tubing.

Lisa cuts a semicircle 1½" (3.8 cm) in from the top edge, ending where the top edge meets the body of the bag. She snips 1¼" (3.2 cm) from the corner on both sides of this freshly cut line, then cuts straight across the flap that connects the snips, finishing with a perpendicular snip in each corner (Figure 3). She repeats this for the other side of the bag.

Lisa stuffs the bag with packing peanuts or discarded bits of bubble wrap until firm to help it retain its shape as it dries. She folds the top flaps inside, brings the top edges together with as little warping as possible, and pins them closed. She pinches a crease in the bag where the handles extend into the body; the tubing will be stitched into the handles and into this crease. She leaves the bag to dry.

Incorporate the tubing in the self-handles

Lisa cuts the tubing in half and places the center of one piece on the center of one handle. Using a needle threaded with 48" (122 cm) of waxed linen, she begins stitching from the center, allowing half the thread to hang loose (tail) for stitching the other half. She pushes the needle through the felt ¼" (6 mm) from each edge, pulling the edges together with whipstitches spaced ¼" (6 mm) apart (Figure 4). When half of one handle is stitched, she stitches the other half. She repeats the procedure on other handle.

Having centered the tubing, the ends come to the same point inside the body of the bag. Balancing the location of the handles on the front and back, Lisa stitches around the bottom of the tube, then passes the linen to the inside. Turning each corner inside out, she ties off the thread, hiding the end in the felt.

Insert magnetic closure

Lisa traces the outline of the magnets onto scrap felt, then cuts out shapes ¼" (6 mm) larger than the outlines. Flipping up a flap, she measures 2" (5 cm) from the handle. Centering one magnet at this point on the inside of the flap, she stitches a felt circle over the magnet. She repeats this 2" (5 cm) from the other end of the handle.

She stitches the flap down, careful not to pierce through to the outside of the bag. She attaches the other pair of magnets on the opposite flap, making certain that the magnets attract (not repel) each other.

Steam and shape the bag

Lisa steams the bag and stuffs it to block it to the desired shape. She presses out any crinkles and presses the ends in and brings the magnet closure together. Remove bubble wrap if necessary.

Apply shellac

Lisa wears rubber gloves while brushing the shellac onto the outside of the bag with the natural bristle brush, dampening rather than saturating the surface. The alcohol will evaporate, leaving a thin layer of crystallized shellac in the wool. Test the shellac on a scrap of felt to determine the amount to apply; using too much shellac causes crystals to form on the surface.

Lisa applies shellac to the entire body of the bag, avoiding the handles. She rotates the bag as it dries so that the bottom does not become overly saturated. Before removing the stuffing, she allows the bag to dry completely. She uses a wire brush to restore the fiber finish to the felt.

Coil-Rimmed Vessel

About the Artist
HEATHER KERNER is a pediatric occupational therapist and the feltmaker behind the company SpiralWorks. Incorporating felt into her coil basketry evolved from her longing for a material that would complement the coils of yarn covered wire. Known for her vessels, Heather also creates felted accessories. She teaches and hosts felting retreats in Canaan, Maine. Her vessels are sold at the New York Sheep and Wool Festival, in galleries, and online.

Heather Kerner debuted her vessels at the New York Sheep and Wool Festival in 2001. Her tasteful array of forms, which brought to mind ceramic pots and gourd baskets, married basketry techniques with felt and created a buzz that weekend.

This earthy brown vessel, whose undulating organic shape casts soft shadows on its own surface, is adorned with soft felt flowers and leaves, depicting tender harbingers of spring. Coil basketry techniques provide a firm, distinctive rim. This vessel honors the passing of seasons, containing hopes for the one to come and remembrances of the one to pass.

Key Techniques

- *Felt around a balloon*
- *Shape the base and undulations*
- *Coil basketry rim*
- *Embellish with flowers and leaves*

Materials

- 4 oz (240 g) C1 Norwegian-blend wool for vessel
- 1 oz (120 g) C1 Norwegian-blend wool in two colors (for flower)
- 2 yd (1.8 m) aluminum 17-gauge electric fence wire
- Several yards variegated wool yarn
- Chenille stick (also known as pipe cleaner)
- Button
- Sewing thread to match C1 wool

In Heather's Studio

- Shallow bucket large enough to accommodate the work and mat
- Textured car mat or sheet of corrugated plastic shelf liner to fit bottom of bucket
- Liquid dish soap
- Balloon
- ½ oz (15 ml) white vinegar
- 2 pairs pantyhose with as much Lycra as possible (such as control top)
- Sharp, pointed scissors (such as spring-action Fiskars)
- Large kitchen spoon or ladle
- Darning or other yarn needle
- Sewing needle
- Empty 32 oz (.95 l) plastic container (such as a yogurt container)
- Bamboo skewer
- Pencil
- Masking or Scotch tape
- Kettle or steamer

Finished measurements

11" (28 cm) tall; 8" (20.5 cm) at widest diameter; 4½" (11.5 cm) diameter and 14" (35.5 cm) circumference at the opening and base.

Hazards of working underwater

Heather cautions that a felter given to lapses into reverie risks the wet wool pooling and drooping beneath the pantyhose. To avoid this hazard, sprinkle the wool-covered balloon with hot soapy water, rolling and pressing it against the textured-bottom basin without the gallon of water. The wool must be wet but need not be submerged.

Prepare to felt

Heather lines the shallow bucket with the textured mat, then fills it with a gallon (3.8 l) of boiling water and adds 1 tablespoon (15 ml) of dish soap. The mixture cools to the desired temperature while she prepares to felt the vessel.

Felt around a balloon

Heather felts around a balloon in place of a ball. After blowing up the balloon to approximate the volume of the desired vessel, she ties a knot at the neck, which will indicate the top of the vessel. She holds the balloon with the knot down and tapes the knot to the worktable.

Heather follows the procedure for felting around a ball, with a few modifications. She prevents a saggy bottom by covering the base of the vessel with crossed strips of wool (Figure 1) before wrapping the entire surface with wool. She chooses pantyhose with a high Lycra content, as they are easier to remove even when the wool is felted in place more than intended. With her hands held wide open, she presses and rolls the wool-covered balloon against the textured bottom of the basin, where the texture acts like an opposing pair of hands.

When the wool has felted, Heather feels for the knot to locate the top of the vessel. She cuts a 4" (10 cm) opening and removes the balloon.

She allows the felt at the edge to remain thick rather than tapered while fulling the vessel against the car mat. Then she squeezes it vigorously under hot water.

She dilutes the vinegar in 1 gallon (3.8 l) of cold water, then submerges the vessel in the mixture before squeezing it again vigorously.

Shape the vessel base

After steaming the bottom over a stream of steam from a boiling kettle or steamer, Heather presses the open end of the yogurt container inside the vessel and pinches the felt around it repeatedly. She repeats the steaming, pressing, and pinching to sculpt the base footprint.

Create undulating ridges

After steaming an imaginary line from top to bottom, Heather uses the kitchen spoon or ladle to press against the steamed area from inside the vessel. She creates undulating ridges and bulbous forms with this technique, steaming and stretching until she is satisfied with the shape.

Form coil basketry rim

Heather centers about a wingspan of yarn on the yarn needle and uses the yarn doubled. She pierces the felt ¼" (6 mm) below the edge and ties the yarn about 4" (10 cm) from the end. She lays one end of the wire along the vessel's edge over the tied-on yarn with the wire extending to the left. While holding the yarn tail along the wire, she wraps the yarn 3 times around the wire and tail, working outward from the tie toward the right (Figure 2). She keeps the wraps close to each other to cover the wire. After wrapping the yarn around the wire 3 or 4 times, she makes a stitch into the felt ¼" (6 mm) from the edge and pulls the yarn tight. She continues until the yarn-covered wire meets around the edge of the vessel.

For the next round and every subsequent round, she continues to wrap and stitch, but she stitches under the previous row instead of the felt (Figure 3).

When the yarn is only 4" (10 cm) long, she removes the needle and threads it with a new wingspan of yarn. Laying the abandoned yarn and a 4" (10 cm) tail of the new yarn along the wire, she begins wrapping again, securing the new and old yarns.

The vessel shown here has 5 rounds of coils. At the end of the wire, she anchors the yarn by threading it behind at least 2 of the coiling stitches inside the basket.

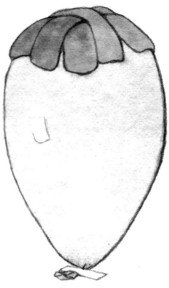

Figure 1. Cover the top of the balloon with crossed strips of wool

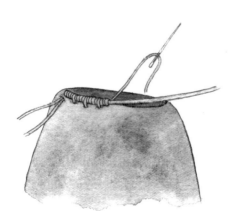

Figure 2. Wrap the yarn around the wire 3 or 4 times, then make a stitch into the felt

Figure 3. When one layer of wire has been covered, begin to stitch under the row below

Coil basketry rim vs wrapped wire rim

In coil basketry, as in this vessel, the wire is wrapped as it is attached, making a stitch into the felt after every 3 or 4 wraps. Floating Poppies (see page 97) also uses a yarn-covered rim, but in that piece the wire is wound with yarn before the covered wire is attached to the felt.

Make and attach floral embellishment

Heather makes felt flowers and leaves for embellishment, then attaches them to the vessel with the button for decoration.

Flower

Heather layers flower-colored wool in about the size and shape of a saucer, then sprinkles it with ¼ cup (60 ml) hot soapy water. She soaps her hands liberally and rubs the wet wool directly, without plastic, pantyhose, or another barrier. Heather rubs the surface of the wet wool for about 5 minutes, then dunks it in hot water and squeezes it vigorously, being careful not to make holes in the delicate fabric. She continues to felt the wool until it is reduced by one-third of the original size. She cuts 5 small wedges from the circle of felt, producing petals, then works the felt for another minute to soften the edge.

Leaf

Heather repeats the process for felting the flower with a 5 x 2" (12.5 x 5 cm) patch of leaf-colored wool. She felts this patch until it measures about 4 x 1" (10 x 2.5 cm). With sewing thread and a sewing needle, Heather makes 7 or 8 whipstitches (see Glossary, page 134) along each long edge to crenellate the felt, transforming it into a leaf. The addition of about 12 short running stitches up the mid-line of the leaf shirrs it slightly, bringing it to life (Figure 4). Heather ties off the thread but doesn't cut it, as it will be used to sew the flower and leaf in place.

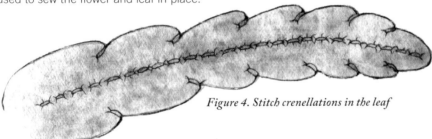

Figure 4. Stitch crenellations in the leaf

Stem

Heather rolls the chenille stick up in a thin layer of wool to completely coat it. She rolls it back and forth on the wet textured surface to felt it, then coils it around a pencil.

Round felt ball

Heather swirls the tip of a skewer in wool until it collects on the end like a Q-tip. She slips the wad of wool off into hot soapy water. Supporting the wet wool in her hand, she lifts it and very gently rolls it in circular motions over the textured mat. (She works without pressure here, as it would cause wrinkles and crevices.) After rolling for a minute or two and allowing the skin to form on the surface, she begins applying increasing pressure for 3 minutes, then rinses and squeezes. Using the threaded sewing needle, she stitches the leaf into place. Then she sews the felt flower and felt ball flower center into place, followed by the button and felted wire.

Scandinavian Boots with Hungarian Flair

About the Artist

PAT SPARK holds an MFA from the University of Washington. Her artwork, including feltmaking, watercolor, monotypes and drawing, is exhibited internationally. She is the author of three books about feltmaking and has contributed to or translated others. Formerly a professor of art, she maintains a scholarly approach to and respect for the traditional and ethnic origins of feltmaking. She teaches workshops in felting and design in her studio, across the United States and internationally. She is editor of the *North American Felters' Network*, a tri-annual publication for felt enthusiasts published by her Fine

Pat Spark uses a closed-template method learned from Hungarian feltmaker Istvan Vidak to make hollow three-dimensional objects in felt. This technique produces felt around an enclosed flat resist; once the object is sufficiently felted, it must be cut open to remove the resist. When researching for her book *Scandinavian-Style Feltmaking*, Pat learned that this technique is also traditional in Norway. Norwegian feltmaker Ruth Johansen taught Pat to make a boot pattern around a person's foot. In this design, Pat shows her appreciation for Istvan and Ruth by combining their techniques in her design. Both boots of the pair are created at once around a single template. Cutting open the felt also separates the boots.

These boots are composed of C1 Norwegian-blend wool fiber, using a Scandinavian pattern and a Hungarian motif for decoration. Combining these international elements honors the interconnectedness of the fiber community.

Key Techniques

- *Make a boot template*
- *Create a seamless join*
- *Open felt to remove resist*
- *Size and shape the boots*
- *Subdue bright color*
- *Needle felt a surface design*
- *Apply soles*

Materials

- 6 oz (180 g) C1 Norwegian-blend wool in main color
- ⅛ oz (5 g) C1 Norwegian-blend wool in each of 5 accent colors
- Upholstery thread to match main color
- One pair shoe soles

In Pat's Studio

- 2 plastic-coated foam placemats
- Duct tape
- 3–4 sheets 18 × 24" (45.5 × 61 cm) newspaper
- Waterproof marker
- Ruler
- Scissors
- Needle
- Towel
- Olive oil or glycerine soap
- 10 black tea bags
- Vinegar
- Cellulose sponge
- 36" (91.5 cm) square nylon mosquito netting
- 18" (45.5 cm) wooden closet rod or 1½" (3.8 cm) diameter PVC pipe
- 18 × 36" (45.5 × 91.5 cm) bamboo mat or bubble wrap
- Washboard (preferably glass)
- Shoe lasts (if the recipient's feet are not available)
- Lightweight plastic sheeting in a color that contrasts with the fleece
- 36-gauge felting needles
- Foam surface for needle felting
- Dinner plate

Note: Shoe lasts, forms shaped like a human foot, are used in making or repairing shoes.

Finished dimensions

11" (28 cm) long; 5" (12.5 cm) wide; 7" (18 cm) tall.

Make the boot pattern and resist

After tracing the outline of the foot or shoe last on the newspaper, Pat draws a line that bisects this outline lengthwise, extending the line beyond the ends. She draws a larger oval about 1½–2" (3.8 to 5 cm) around the outline. (This larger outline is necessary for proper sizing.) She cuts out the oval, folds it in half widthwise, and draws a line on this fold.

After tracing the oval on another piece of newspaper, she draws 3 lines: a 6" (15 cm) line straight up from the heel, another up from the intersection of cross-marks, and a line across the top. To finish the pattern, she draws a curved line from the center of the line above the outline toward the toe. She cuts out this single-boot pattern.

Pat traces the pattern onto a large sheet of newspaper. To produce a conjoined boot pattern, she rotates the pattern (to avoid making two left feet) and flips it over, aligning the boot tops (Figure 1). She designed this interlocking pattern so that the high part of one boot would be the low part of the other.

Pat uses duct tape to join the two short edges of the placemats. After cutting out the pattern, she traces it on both the joined placemat and the lightweight plastic. Cutting out these two tracings, she has a template thick enough to feel within the wool when used as the resist and a waterproof pattern to direct her wool placement.

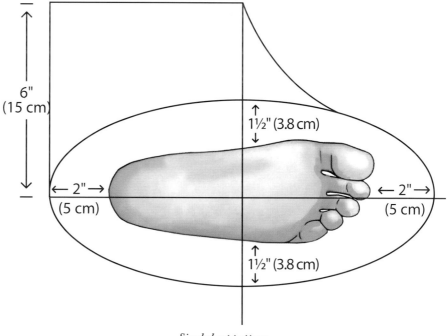

Single boot pattern

Place wool on pattern

Pat divides the main color of wool into two portions. She lays the plastic sheeting pattern on the bamboo mat and places one portion of wool in 4 perpendicular layers that extend 1½" (3.8 cm) beyond the edges of the pattern. She covers the wool with netting and uses the sponge to press soapy water into it. When all the fiber is wet and the air bubbles have been expelled, she removes the netting and centers the template on the wool. She folds the fringed edges up over the top of the template (Figure 2). She repeats the layering with the second portion of wool, now using the wet wool-coated template as the pattern. Again using the netting and sponge, she wets down the wool. To ensure seamless edges, she turns it over, smoothing the edges up over the wool-covered template.

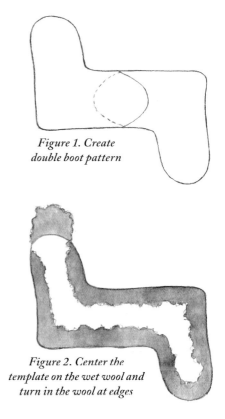

Figure 1. Create double boot pattern

Figure 2. Center the template on the wet wool and turn in the wool at edges

Make seamless joins

Pat needs to be sure that the wool wrapped over the edge of the resist stays put. (If it moves outward, flanges will develop.) Pat covers the wool-encased resist with mosquito netting, tucking it under tightly at the edges, where it functions in the same way as the pantyhose over a ball (Figure 3).

With lavishly soaped hands, Pat rubs along the edge of the wool and resist. She presses from the outside edge of the template towards the center, slowly massaging the boots with flat hands. She periodically lifts the netting to prevent it from felting into the fleece.

She massages the boots for about 10 minutes. She continues rubbing through the net until the wool on both sides feels firm and tight.

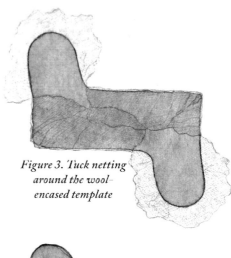

Figure 3. Tuck netting around the wool-encased template

Full the boots

Pat warms the boots (still wrapped in netting) before continuing, either by using tongs to dip them into simmering soapy water or by putting them in the microwave on high for a couple of minutes. When the boots cool to a temperature she can handle, she rolls them up in the bamboo mat with the closet rod and continues to full them until they have shrunk noticeably and the template buckles.

Open the felt and separate the boots

Referring to the newspaper pattern, Pat cuts one side first, snipping down to but not through the template (Figure 4). After making the offset cut, she turns the boots over and cuts the second side.

She massages the cut area to strengthen it before pulling out the resist, then turns the boots inside out to work the interior in the same way as the exterior.

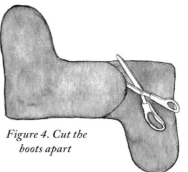

Figure 4. Cut the boots apart

Size, rinse, and shape the boots

Pat turns the boots right-side out and puts them on the feet or lasts. Evaluating which areas need to be shrunk, she heats an area, then rubs it against the washboard or slaps it against the table. She continues until the boots are the correct size. Pat rinses out the soap and subdues the bright plum color of these boots by simmering the boots in a kettle of water with ½ cup (120 ml) vinegar and 10 tea bags for 20 minutes. When she is satisfied with the color, she allows the boots to dry in the desired shape, ideally on the form.

Felt surface design

Pat allows the boots to dry thoroughly before using a felting needle to apply a motif that recalls traditional Hungarian felt. She lays the boot flap right-side up on the foam needle-felting surface. She sketches the motif in color and arranges several puffs of wool in those colors on a plate.

To make each shape, she places wisps of fiber on an area of the boots slightly larger than the desired shape. She pokes the needle into the fiber, tracing the outside edge of the shape. By folding the excess fiber over the inside, she produces a sharply defined edge. Rapid shallow pokes overall help anchor the fiber. To outline areas, she pulls strips of the darker fiber and taps just a few fibers at their ends into place. Then, working only a few millimeters at a time, she needles the outline into place.

Pat also wet felts the needle-felted motif. She presses hot soapy water into the area with the cellulose sponge, covers it with netting, and rubs, working both the top and underside of the flap before rinsing and towel drying.

Apply the soles

Pat applies the soles according to the manufacturer's directions (see Sources, page 140).

Transition Felt Hat

About the Artist

JACKIE MIRABEL pursued hand-craft in her free time while working in the corporate world. Upon retiring in 2002, she created Mirabel Naturals, her jewelry and felt fashion business.

Jackie Mirabel's stylish hats, though tempered by a refined elegance, convey a sense of humor. She creates pieces that project a sense of fun and style with a bit of sophistication. Dramatic shapes, frequently employing multiple folds and pleats, are characteristic of her work. Her application of color intensifies the drama of her shapes and forms. She uses rich, high-value tones, subtle designs in prefelt, and crisp graphics through layered cutouts. When thinking of her hats, she often keeps in mind a quotation from British journalist Katharine Whitehorn: "I have recently acquired a new hat of such ferocity that it has been running my whole life for me. I wake up in the morning thinking, *who shall I wear my hat at today?*"

Key Techniques

- *Make a custom beret resist*
- *Decorate a surface with layered cutouts and inlaid fabric*
- *Shape a beret opening*

Materials

- 1 oz (28 g) solid-colored merino in main color
- ½ oz (14 g) solid merino in each of 5 accent colors
- 3 scraps of chiffon or other open-weave fabric, each about 6 × 2" (15 × 5 cm)
- 24" (60 cm) fleece tape (available from a craft or sewing store)
- Sewing thread

In Jackie's Studio

- Olive oil soap
- 3 squares bubble wrap (one 3" [91.5 cm] square, one 28" [71 cm] square, one 8" [20.5 cm] square)
- Permanent marker
- 2 pieces 40" (101.5 cm) square plastic sheeting
- 2 stretchy ties made from knee-high stockings
- Sewing needle
- Steam iron or kettle
- Wooden hat block
- Straight pins
- Sharp-pointed scissors

Finished measurements

17" (43 cm) long; 11" (28 cm) wide; 5.5" (14 cm) tall.

Make a beret-style hat resist

Jackie draws an outline of the hat on the smooth side of the 28" (71 cm) square of bubble wrap, which she'll cut to form a resist. She starts by marking 2 lines, one 6" (15 cm) in from one edge and the other 11" (28 cm) from the opposite edge with an X at its midpoint. She tapes 1" (2.5 cm) of a 12" (30.5 cm) piece of thread to the marker and tacks the other end of the thread to the X. Holding the marker vertical, she draws a circle 22" (56 cm) in diameter. To transform the resist to a comma shape, Jackie draws a curved point along 8" (20.5 cm) of the circumference that extends 6" (15 cm). She finishes drawing the "comma" resist (see below), marking the opening, and cuts it out.

Prefelt leaves and chiffon scraps

Like most feltmakers, Jackie maintains a stash of prefelts and open-weave fabrics, sometimes scraps from previous projects. For this project, she makes prefelt from one of the accent colors of wool, then cuts leaf shapes from the prefelt. She also cuts snippets of silk chiffon, setting these aside to place on the hat.

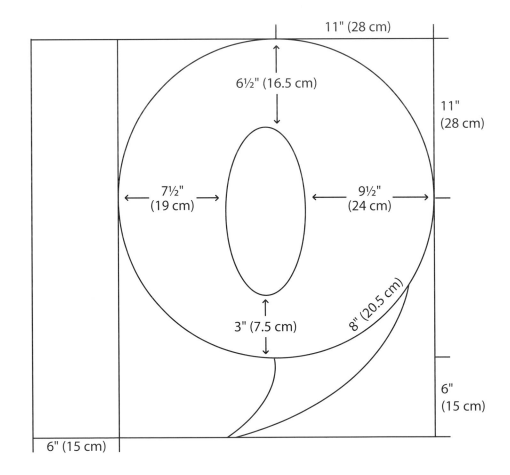

Comma resist

Create layered felt

Jackie trims and rounds the corners of the 8" (20.5 cm) square of bubble wrap to form a surface-design resist. She centers the beret resist on a sheet of plastic, which is in turn placed on the smooth side of the largest (and only remaining) square of bubble wrap. Jackie builds 2 perpendicular layers of wool in a patch at least 1" (2.5 cm) larger than the rounded 8" (20.5 cm) resist, using a color that will contrast with the hat's exterior (Figure 1). She wets the patch, covers it with plastic, and gently rubs it for 5 minutes. After removing the plastic, she centers the rounded 8" (20.5 cm) resist on top of the patch of wool.

Layer wool on the comma resist

Ignoring the patch and smaller resist for now, Jackie builds 4 thin even perpendicular layers of wool for the top of the beret, blending and layering colors as desired. The layers of wool extend 1" (2.5 cm) beyond the edges of the comma resist. She dampens the wool evenly with warm soapy water, covers the piece in plastic, and rubs for several minutes to partially felt it.

Place prefelts and chiffon surface design

Jackie removes the plastic sheeting and arranges the pieces of prefelt and chiffon on the surface. She replaces the plastic sheeting and rubs the surface some more.

Layer wool for bottom of beret

Jackie lifts the plastic sheet and "sandwich" of the resist, wool, and plastic off the large square of bubble wrap. She flips them over onto the bubble wrap. Gently removing the plastic, she turns the outside edges of the wool over the top of the resist and eases the wool around curves to avoid forming bumps. She places 3 perpendicular layers of wool on the surface, extending the wool at least 1" (2.5 cm) beyond the edge of the comma resist but avoiding the center of the oval, marked as the opening.

Figure 1. Layer a patch of wool under the surface-design resist

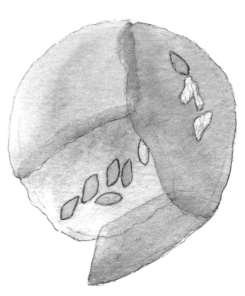

Figure 2. Place surface design

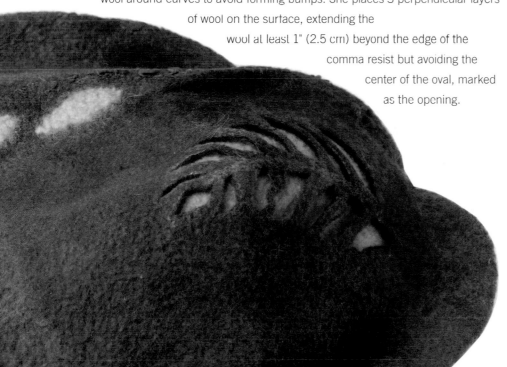

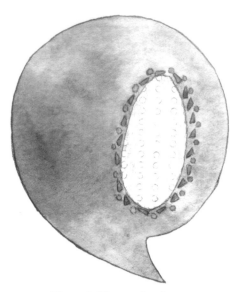

*Figure 3. Place surface design
around the hat opening*

Design the beret opening

Jackie places most of the fourth layer of wool in the area surrounding the opening (an area she indicated on the resist). Using dots of fiber and triangles cut from prefelt, she decorates the area. When she is satisfied with the arrangement, she wets the area, covers it with plastic, and rubs it for 5 minutes. Then she rolls up the piece within the bubble wrap and felts it.

Cut a motif in the layered felt

After the hat is felted, Jackie marks a leaf design into the top surface of the hat above the colored patch and 8" (20.5 cm) resist. She snips into the marks, being careful not to penetrate the bubble wrap beneath, and cuts away the design. If possible, she carefully pulls the resist through a cutout. If she deems the design too fragile or the cutouts too small, she approaches from the interior, cutting a slit in the patch from beneath the resist and removes it from there.

Cut the beret opening

To cut the opening after felting is complete, Jackie refers to the triangle and dot surface design she used to outline the opening. She removes the comma resist, then fulls the hat to the desired size.

Shape and size the hat

The hat should be fulled to slightly smaller than the block. Steaming the hat allows it to stretch over the block. The fulled felt is thin and supple, yielding easily to the several folds and creases Jackie pinches into it. She steams and pinches the folds, pinning them in place while the hat dries.

With wrong sides together, Jackie attaches fleece bias tape around the interior of the opening. Using small whipstitches, she sews along the lower edge of the tape and edge of hat.

Roll in a towel

For a drier and tidier felting experience, Jackie rolls the piece in and around a towel. Rolling the work around a rolled-up towel confines the water expelled in the rolling phase and provides a soft and yielding core. Wrap the rolled project up in another towel before securing it with ties.

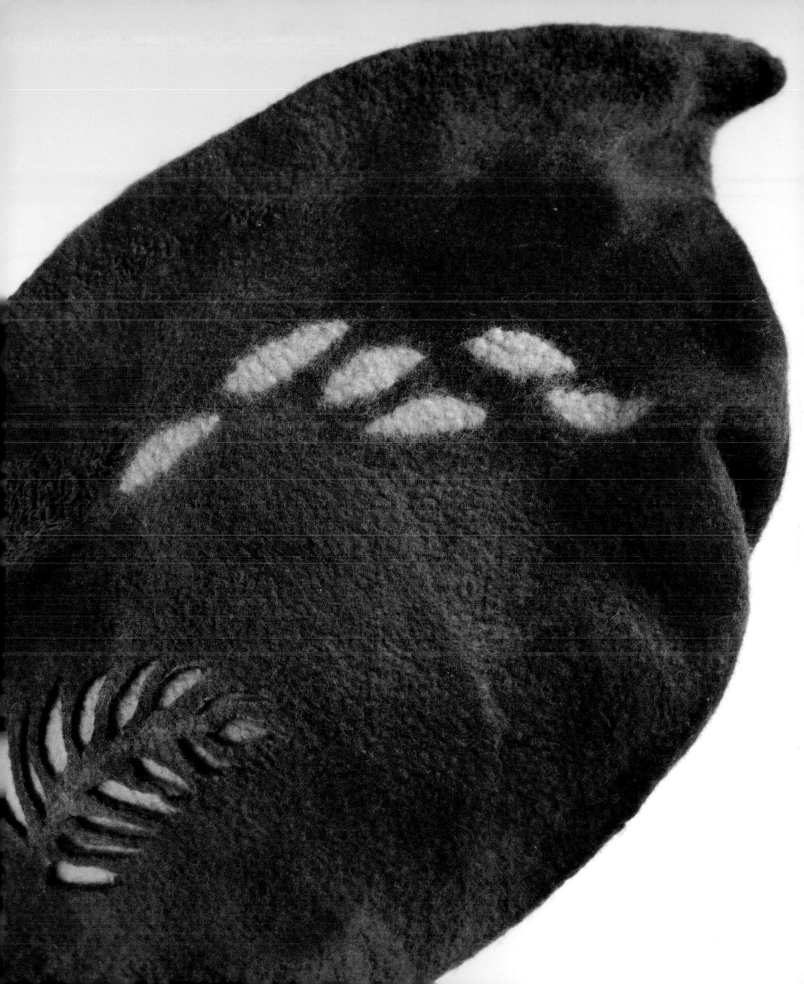

Zabuton Meditation Cushion

About the Artist
Theresa May-O'Brien studied with legendary watercolorist Jack Flynn. When her focus shifted to feltmaking, she lived in Scandinavia, Kyrgyzstan, Hungary, and Turkey, where she studied with master feltmakers, learning both the methods and the culture of the felting tradition. Her mentorship under feltmaker Mehmet Girgic instilled an appreciation for Turkish textiles and honed her skills. They subsequently developed a shared business selling Turkish felting items including wool, soap, and mats. Theresa teaches the craft of feltmaking and the cultural bridges that can be built through art. She lives on a small farmstead in upstate New York.

Theresa May-O'Brien has always found inspiration in the beauty of her surroundings. Having enjoyed recognition as a landscape artist, creative inquiry led her from watercolor to fiber, where she applies the eye of a painter to feltmaking.

Her fluency in Turkish feltmaking design and technique informs her work, as in this meditation cushion that displays the outlined and colorful lotus flower "Zantra," a meaningful motif for yoga practitioners. To produce an opening that requires no button or zipper, she uses overlapping resists. To impart a pebbled texture and subtle color blends, Theresa layers wool that differs in both type and color.

Key Techniques

- *Outline a surface design with a cartoon and clear resist*
- *Overlap resists for buttonless opening*

Materials

- 2 oz (60 g) total C1 Norwegian-blend wool (sample includes 7 colors)
- 3 oz (90 g) total solid-colored merino, divided in 2 portions
- 6 oz (180 g) Turkish natural white merino roving, divided in 2 portions
- 1 oz (30 g) Turkish black fattail wool 20 × 40" (51 × 102 cm) square piece of cotton fabric
- 16 oz (480 g) cotton stuffing (available at sewing or quilting stores)
- Sewing thread

In Theresa's Studio

- 31" (79 cm) square paper
- 31" (79 cm) square clear bubble wrap
- 15 × 29" (38 × 73.5 cm) bubble wrap
- 36 × 72" (91.5 × 183 cm) felting mat
- 36 × 72" (91.5 × 183 cm) sheet of plastic
- Tape or straight pins
- Pen, colored pens, and black marker
- Scissors
- Ruler, tape measure
- Pool noodle
- 3 pantyhose legs
- Olive oil soap
- Towels
- Small bucket
- Corn whiskbroom

Finished measurements

22" (56 cm) square; 2" (5 cm) deep.

Theresa's felting mat

A textured mat is part of every feltmaker's studio. Theresa uses a sort of hybrid, a plastic "grass" woven mat similar to a kind of beach blanket.

Make and place a cartoon of the surface design

Tapestry weavers mount a full-scale drawing of the proposed piece, called a cartoon, behind the vertical warp on the loom, as a guide for weaving the design. To apply this concept to feltmaking, Theresa draws her design to true scale on the paper. When she is pleased with the outcome, she traces the pattern in black marker to be visible through the bubble wrap, which she uses as the resist.

She places her felting mat on the table, allowing half of it to hang over the edge, and covers it with a sheet of plastic. She pins or tapes the pattern to the underside of the resist so that the motif shows through. After centering the resist, she begins to place the fiber.

Arrange fiber for surface design

Theresa divides the black wool into thin strips like pencil roving. To control their thickness, she drafts the fibers lengthwise and rolls them slightly. She dunks a strip of the black pencil roving into the soapy water, lifts it, and lets it drip, but avoids wringing or twisting it. She finds that wet wool makes a sharper outline and clings to the resist.

Figure 1. Outline and then fill in the motif with wool

Starting at the center, she works outward, following the pattern that shows through and overlapping the ends of the roving for evenness. She fills in the lotus flower and the corner triangles with colored C1 as though coloring in a coloring book (Figure 1).

To produce the subtle rings in the area around the lotus flower, she wraps a bit of green or brown fiber around a finger, then rolls it off. She places several rings in this way before filling in the area with wisps of colored roving. Building the felt from the inside out, she covers the motif with thin wisps of the half of the colored roving for the pillow top.

She crosses this layer with perpendicular wisps of roving, permitting them to extend 1½" (3.8 cm) beyond the edge of the resist. This will form the seamless join of front and back, making the pillow three-dimensional.

She wets the wool before covering it with plastic and rubbing. When wetting the work, Theresa is careful to disperse the water uniformly without disturbing the wool. She dips a corn whiskbroom into the bucket of hot soapy water and shakes the water onto her wool.

Once the wool is wet, she covers the work with a plastic sheet and rubs the surface.

Flip the work without lifting it from the mat

Theresa folds the hanging half of the felting mat up over the work, then flips over the folded mat and its contents.

She folds back this half of the felting mat and plastic sheet and removes the paper pattern from the resist. She turns up the roving that extends along the edge of the resist and fills in any thin spots to ensure an even and seamless join.

Seamless vs flanged

Ruffled flange edge

A flange is the edge that results when the top layers and bottom layers of wool have felted together beyond the edge of the resist. Unlike slippers, mittens, most hats, and other three-dimensional items made by wrapping the wool around the edge of the resist, a flange can be desirable on a pillow. For a 3" (7.5 cm) ruffled flange, work 3" (7.5 cm) beyond the resist, layering wool in a 37" (94 cm) square.

Figure 2. Place fiber over two-thirds of the cushion bottom

Figure 3. Place the resist

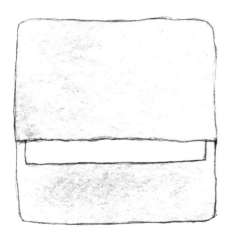

Figure 4. Cover two-thirds from the opposite edge over the resist

Overlap the resist for a buttonless opening

Theresa divides each portion of the reserved roving in half again. Envisioning the bottom divided in thirds, she uses one-half of the remaining colored roving to place a layer of vertical wisps on the lower two-thirds, avoiding the top third (Figure 2). She layers horizontal wisps of one-half of the Turkish roving over the colored roving allowing the wool to extend ½" (1.3 cm) over the pillow edge. She wets the wool, covers it with plastic, and rubs it all over as before. She replaces the plastic with the overlap resist so that it covers the top half of the roving just placed and extends onto the resist (Figure 3).

She covers the exposed two-thirds of the pillow with colored roving aligned vertically out to the sides (Figure 4). She crosses this layer with a perpendicular layer of the remaining Turkish roving, being certain that the fiber extends ½" (1.3 cm) past the top edge for a good join.

The wool that overlaps in the middle third is separated by the resist.

Felt and full

Theresa puts a CD on and then wets, rubs and, rolls for the duration of two songs. Known for her felt rugs, she is accustomed to "extreme feltmaking" or feltmaking as an aerobic activity. Occasionally she slides a hand inside the pillow at the overlap of the resist, running her fingers along the seam to smooth it.

She felts and fulls the piece until it shrinks to 22" (56 cm) square.

Fill pillow

After the piece dries, Theresa slides a 20" (51 cm) pillow form inside. To make a pillow insert, she folds the cotton fabric in half with right sides together and sews all 3 edges, leaving a 2" (5 cm) opening in one seam. She turns the fabric right side out, fills it with cotton stuffing, and sews the remaining seam closed.

(She could also opt to purchase a ready-made 20" (51 cm) square pillow form.)

Slippers with a Floral Twist

About the Artist

LINDA VAN ALSTYNE has relied on her hands for many years as a physical and occupational therapist practicing body-work. She has always enjoyed working with her hands to create firm material from which to coax three-dimensional forms. To that end, she crocheted and wove free-form baskets until feltmaking stole her heart. In addition to hats, footwear, and ornamental works, she specializes in one-of-a-kind masks, a form she was introduced to by Beth Beede (page 10).

Linda Van Alstyne was swept away by the immediate gratification, endless adventure, and physicality of feltmaking. The natural, earthy, organic, and ancient origins of the medium appealed to her. The give-and-take between the felter and the felt is a subtle and ineffable dance that Linda describes as "sensing when the wool is ready."

Rather than use a hat block, shoe last, or other form, Linda sculpts wool by stretching and fulling until it acquires the right shape and size, and the felt becomes leather-like and hard-as-papier-mâché.

Felting around a pair of simple oval resists yields a pair of perfectly fitted slippers, to which she adds a spike that blooms at the end.

Key Techniques

- *Customize a template resist*
- *Make soap slurry*
- *Use a grid system to monitor layers of wool*
- *Incorporate scrim*
- *Harden, shape, and size slippers*
- *Develop a flower from a spike*

Materials

- C1 Norwegian-blend wool: 8 oz (240 g) for women's sizes 6–8; 9 oz (270 g) for sizes 9–10; 10 oz (300 g) for men's sizes 9–10, 11 oz (330 g) for men's sizes 11–12
- 2 strips of cheesecloth, each measuring 4 × 12" (10 × 30.5 cm)
- Sewing thread in coordinating color

In Linda's Studio

- 12 × 36" (30.5 × 91.5 cm) closed-cell foam or tiny bubble wrap
- 30 × 60" (76 × 152.5 cm) reed or bamboo mat
- 4 sheets of clear plastic from trash can liners, each measuring 20" (51 cm) square
- Permanent marker
- Scissors
- Ruler or tape measure
- Towels
- Washboard or 15 × 18" (38 × 45.5 cm) piece of vinyl stair tread
- 15 × 18" (38 × 45.5 cm) piece of rubber stair tread
- Bar of olive oil soap
- Bonsai watering ball, laundry sprinkle-head bottle, or plastic bottle with holes poked in the lid
- 30 × 36" (76 × 91.5 cm) or larger piece of mosquito netting
- 2 boot or cafeteria trays
- Tape
- 3 ties from pantyhose legs
- Pool noodle
- 4 T-pins or corsage pins
- Drum stick or wooden spoon handle
- Heavy-duty paint stirrer
- Microwave oven or steamer
- Pair of shoe lasts (optional)
- Nonskid fabric coating such as Super Grip
- Tennis ball
- Sewing needle

Finished measurements

10½" (26.5 cm) long; 3¾" (9.5 cm) wide; 3½" (9 cm) high

Customize a resist

Linda folds the bubble wrap in half with the bubbles on the inside, then traces a foot on it to establish the correct size. She draws an oval outline 1½" (3.8 cm) outside the long sides and 1¾" (4.5 cm) from the heel and toe of the foot shape. For the spike that will become a blossom, she draws a 10" (25.5 cm) curved line from the toe that arches up and back towards the heel. She measures about 3" (7.5 cm) down the side of the toe and from there draws an intersecting arc. The spiked edge of the resist becomes the top of the slipper when an opening is created, while the opposite edge becomes the sole.

She secures the folded bubble wrap with tape and cuts out 2 template resists at once.

Make soap slurry

Linda loves using olive oil soap. Like many felters, she makes a "slurry," a bar dissolved in water or grates about ¼ c (6.5 ml) of soap directly into 2 gal (5.2 l) water.

Divide wool

Linda tears the batt into 4" (10 cm) wide arm-length strips. By pinching the surface of a strip, she easily lifts off 4 layers.

Each slipper is constructed of 6 layers of fiber, a resist, and another 6 layers of fiber, or 12 portions of thin strips of wool. From a narrow end, she loosely winds up each thin strip from the first half of the batt and places them on a tray in 12 separate coils, one for each layer. She repeats with the other half of the batt and the second tray.

Use a grid system to monitor layers of wool layers

Linda uses a grid system to monitor her placement of wool. Notice the icon used to convey the direction of wool layer.

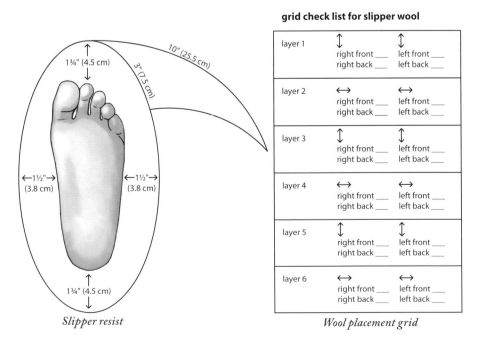

Slipper resist

Wool placement grid

Lay out first layer of fiber

Linda places the mirror-image templates on the mat flanked by the 2 trays of coiled wool (Figure 1). As she uses each portion, she checks off the corresponding section of the grid.

The first layer will be on the outside of the finished slippers, so Linda considers the decorative elements as she places them to extend over the patterns' edges. This brings the design around to the other side and prevents an interruption down the center of the slipper (Figure 2). The spike, being so narrow, is finicky, so Linda uses a thin strip of batt and wraps the wool tight around the tapered end.

She dampens this design with sprinkles of soapy water (water with a little slurry stirred in) without disturbing it. (A Bonsai watering ball from Germany is her preferred tool for this.) Placing the sheet of plastic on top, she presses out the air and spreads the water throughout the wool.

Linda carefully turns the wet and woolly resists over. She folds the wool that extends beyond the resist up over the top and presses it toward the center of the resist. She places the decorative wool on this side and once again wets, covers, presses, and flips the pieces.

She covers each resist with one portion of wool in a thin and even layer that extends ½" (1.3 cm) beyond. Again she wets, covers, presses, and flips them before folding the wool along the edge up sharply. Each time she folds the wool up along the edge, she gently rubs the edges with soapy hands, pressing vertically into the edge and inward toward the center. She covers this other side of each resist with a portion. All 4 sides for Layer 1 should be checked off on the grid.

Place two more layers on each side

Linda repeats layering fiber on both sides of the resists 2 more times, for a total of 3 layers of wool on each slipper. She places each layer perpendicular to the one beneath it, coaxing the wool back toward the center of the resist each time she flips it to prevent the wool from slumping off the edge as it grows thicker.

Insert cheesecloth scrim

After completing 6 full portions, Linda places cheesecloth on the bottom of each slipper. She positions each piece so that half runs lengthwise along the edge opposite the spike, while the other half hangs ready to be placed on the other side of the slippers (Figure 3). Cheesecloth "scrim" in the sole area prolongs the wear of the slippers.

She places the seventh portion of wool on top of the cheesecloth. Since she is no longer wrapping the spike, she uses the extra wool on the sole area of the slipper. After turning the pieces over, she pulls the cheesecloth up and eases it into place on this side. (Wrinkles are okay, but folds are not.)

Place remaining layers of wool

Consulting her grid, Linda applies the remaining layers of wool over the cheesecloth, still perpendicular to the layers beneath. Ripples may develop in the layers of wool; she adds another layer right on top of them.

Figure 1. Position templates and trays of wool

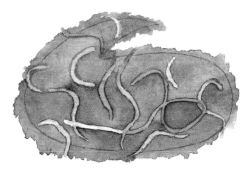

Figure 2. Layer wool on resist

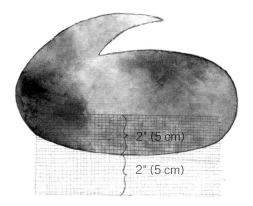

2" (5 cm)

2" (5 cm)

Figure 3. Place cheesecloth on top of third layer of wool in sole area

3"
(7.5 cm)

2"
(5 cm)

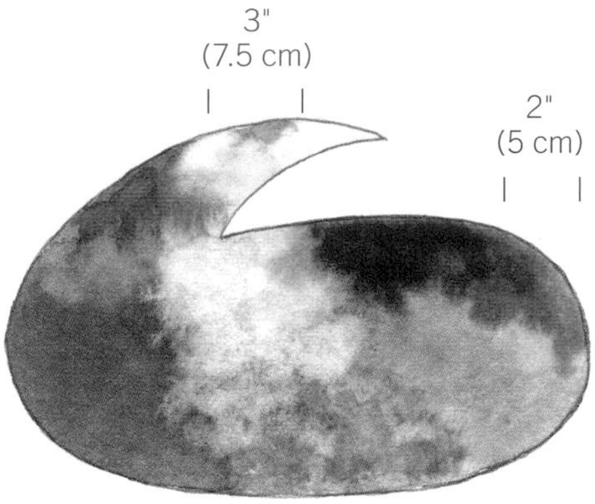

Figure 4. Cut the opening

Firm the resist edges, soles, and spikes

Linda substitutes mosquito netting for the plastic covering the wet wool and works each slipper individually. She wets and soaps both hands and gently cups them along the edge of the slipper. She moves her hands gently along the edges, pressing almost indiscernibly inward.

As the edges firm, she starts to work up over the top of the resists toward the center. With a light touch, she slides her hands over the slipper package without moving the netting or fiber. She thoroughly works this side, working the wool right up to the edge of the resist but not beyond. She turns the piece over, covers it with netting, and works this side thoroughly. She carefully inspects the edges during the felting process to prevent a flange or crease from forming.

When both sides and the edges are firm, she gently works each spike between her hands, rolling it back and forth until firm. When they pass the pinch test she continues to felt the pair by rolling them up in the mat around a pool noodle, securing the roll with pantyhose ties. Every few minutes she unrolls the mat and rotates the pieces 90 degrees to work them from all directions. To check the edges for a potential crease, she stands each on its sole edge (scrim area) and grasps the two sides of the slipper and pulls them apart. If she sees a crease forming, she eliminates it by rubbing it vigorously with the bar of soap, then tugging the sides and pressing the crease flat along the mat.

Cut the opening

She snips a tiny slit into the top edge of each slipper about 3" (7.5 cm) from the base of the spike, then continues to cut along an imaginary line perpendicular to the endpoint of the sole where it lifts to become the heel (Figure 4). (This is usually about 2" [5 cm] from the end of the slipper.) Before continuing to cut, she checks that the incision will be centered. She cuts the second slipper to match, then pulls out the template and gently stretches the opening from side to side rather than toe to heel.

Full the slippers

Linda places a slipper on its sole parallel to the ridges of the vinyl stair tread or washboard. While flattening it, she rolls it into a long bundle from one edge of the sole to the other. She rolls this bundle back and forth over the ridges without rubbing 25 to 35 times, then unrolls it and rerolls from the opposite edge 25 to 35 times more.

Stretch the slippers

Before stretching and pulling the slipper from toe to heel and side to side, Linda heats each one with steam or 1 minute in the microwave oven. Heat loosens the fibers by expanding the air spaces between them, allowing her to pull the fibers in the opposite direction. When she resumes fulling, the fibers travel back to where they were and even farther—this is the key to hardening and shaping the felt.

Invert the spike

Before continuing to full, Linda prepares the spike by snipping the end off and running a drumstick or dowel through it. She turns the spike so that the outside is now inside the slipper and continues fulling. Working the slipper side to side, she applies increasing pressure.

Rest and resume fulling

Linda usually takes a break, allowing the wool (and herself) to rest before returning with hot water for about 2 more hours of aggressive work ahead.

She rolls the heated slipper forward at a 45-degree angle from the heel, up to the center. Done from both sides, this shapes an arch.

Beat slippers with a stick

In place of throwing, as some felters do, Linda prefers to beat the felt with a heavy paint stirring stick so that she can target specific areas to harden and shape. Holding the slipper in a way to prevent whacking herself, she beats each side of the slipper with the flat side of a stick 20 or 30 times in each direction. She turns the slipper over and beats the sole, concentrating on the center area to harden the arch.

She turns the slippers right-side out, finally able to appreciate the surface design she began with, and continues fulling. She stretches the heated slippers against plastic or wooden cooking spoons that are held inside or pressing the felt over the spoons. She repeats alternating between heating and stretching the pieces. When stretching the sole lengthwise, she works only the flat central area. She heats and stretches the heel over a tennis ball or similar shape. Once she has attained the desired width, she rolls them aggressively from heel to toe, checking the progress frequently.

The top of the slipper near the spike is sometimes underdone. Working from inside, Linda presses that area against the ridges of the mat and vibrates the wool there by moving her hand in an exaggerated tremble.

Develop a flower from the spike

Linda heats the spike if necessary, then pushes it to the outside with the drumstick.

She makes 5 lengthwise cuts into the spike, opening it into 5 petals (Figure 5). She felts the cut edges before twisting the spike until it curls onto the slipper with the flower open on top and pins it in place. When it is dry, she removes the pins and secures the flower position with a needle and thread, adding a bead to the center for decoration.

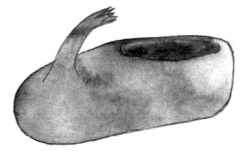

Figure 5. Snip the spike and open into petals

Finish the slippers

Shoe lasts can be used to keep the slippers in shape while they dry. A nonslip sole can be achieved by painting the heel and toe area of the sole with 2 or 3 coats of Super Grip (best done outdoors).

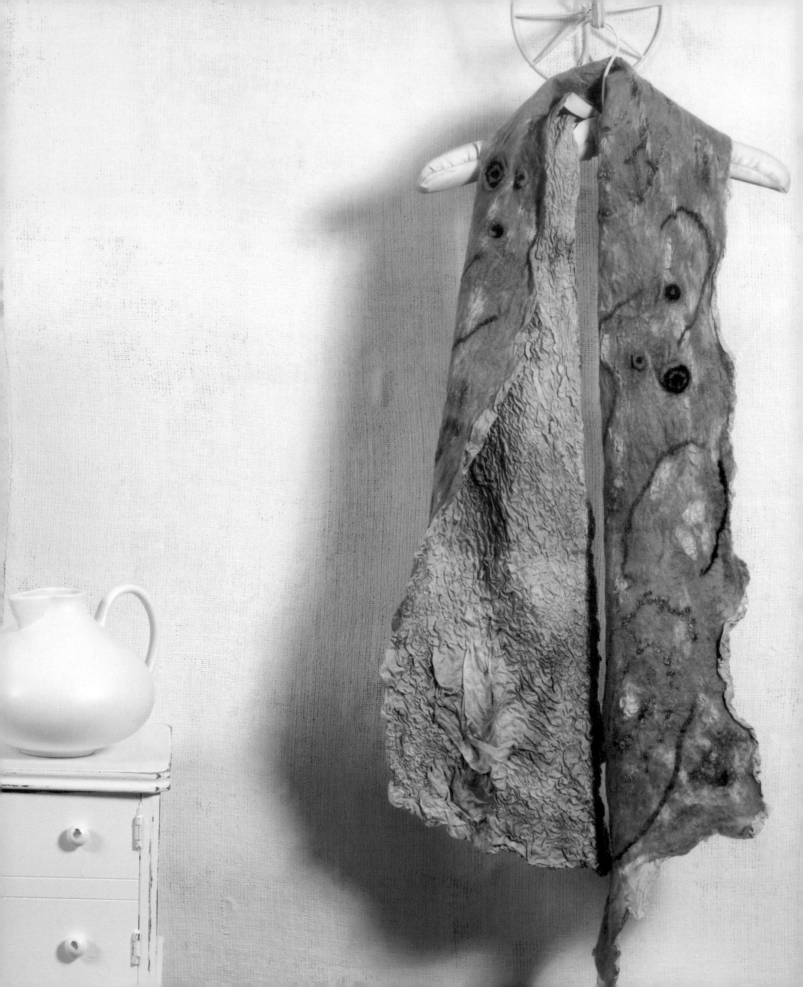

Gossamer Saffron Scarf

About the Artist
ELIZABETH BUCHTMAN is a
gardener, soapmaker, beadworker,
crocheter, knitter, and feltmaker. She
works with polymer clay, Precious Metal
Clay, beadwork, and gemstones in her
jewelry designs. A dedicated space she
calls her "craft room" boasts several
projects in progress. In the kitchen, she
puts up her own preserves, pickles, jellies,
and even occasionally some dandelion
wine. She offers her scarves, felt bags, and
children's art-to-wear at local craft shows
and on her website. She also teaches
children to craft and felt in schools and
after-school programs.

Elizabeth Buchtman has a deep and abiding regard for craft,
especially felt, which offers her a full spectrum of form through
fabric, structural and sculptural techniques, and color. This
project combines wool and silk, both protein fibers that are easily
dyed in a microwave oven. She paints white silk fabric with three
colors of dye that denote the energy and warmth of the sun, and
then felts a thin layer of wool into it, working from a palette of
six colors. Draped over the shoulders and paired with a sleeveless
dress, this gossamer felt scarf keeps an evening chill at bay, like
a warm embrace.

Key Techniques

- *Dye protein fiber*
- *Felt into silk*

Materials

- 2½ oz (75 g) solid-colored merino, divided among 6 colors
- 1 yd (91.5 cm) silk chiffon fabric 42" (106.5 cm) wide
- Yarn
- ½ oz (15 g) mohair locks
- White sewing thread
- 3 colors Jacquard Procion MX Dyes

In Elizabeth's Studio

- 24 × 90" (61 × 229 cm) bubble wrap
- 24 × 90" (61 × 229 cm) nylon sheer curtain
- 24 × 90" (61 × 229 cm) plastic sheet
- 2 knee-high stockings or legs cut from pantyhose
- 40-gauge or other fine felt needle
- 2" (5 cm) thick or larger foam needle-felting surface
- 2' (61 cm) pipe insulation
- 3 disposable cups
- 3 sponge brushes
- 2 white can liners
- 2 ziplock bags, one sandwich size and one gallon size
- Plastic juice reamer
- Towels
- Scissors
- Sewing needle or sewing machine
- Microwave oven
- Latex or rubber gloves
- Dr. Bronner's Lavender Pure-Castile soap

Finished measurements

10" (25.5 cm) wide; 70" (178 cm) long.

Two at once!

Split lengthwise, a 2 yd (183 cm) length of fabric makes 2 scarves without sewing. Lay out 1 scarf as given at right, wet it, rub it, and top it with plastic. Lay out the second scarf on top, then work both scarves at once!

Cool-water felting

Avoid using hot water when felting wool into a fabric base. Hot water expedites felting, which will cause the wool to felt to itself, forming a layer separate from the fabric. Cool water slows the process to allow the wool to work into the fabric while felting.

Prepare the silk background

Elizabeth cuts the silk fabric in half widthwise and machine-stitches the ends together, yielding an 18 x 84" (45.5 x 213 cm) piece. Before dyeing, she launders the silk to remove sizing or fixatives that could adversely affect the process. She doesn't dry it before proceeding to dye.

Dye the fabric

Elizabeth cuts open the can liners and uses them to cover and protect her worktable. She smooths the wet silk onto the plastic. She follows the package instructions for Jacquard Procion MX Dyes, stirring 1 tsp (5 ml) of dye powder into ⅓ cup (80 ml) of warm water in each of 3 disposable cups to yield 3 dyes.

Using a sponge brush, she paints the silk with the lightest color. She overdyes some of the painted area by painting a darker color over a lighter one, then gingerly dabs some patches of the third dye. To keep the colors variegated, she doesn't over-work the dyeing.

When she is satisfied with the color, she folds the silk and places it in the smaller ziplock bag. She seals the bag and places it in the microwave oven. As she cooks it on high for 15 seconds, the bag expands with steam.

She carefully opens the bag, aware that the contents are very hot, and allows steam to escape before resealing the bag and heating it for an additional 15 seconds. The contents are now very hot indeed. She opens the bag carefully and places it under cold running water until the silk is cool enough to handle. Removing the silk from the bag, she runs cold water through it until the water runs clear.

Arrange and wet wool on silk

Elizabeth smooths the silk onto the smooth side of the bubble wrap. She places wool as surface design on the silk fabric, arranging fine wisps of fiber on the surface without regard for direction (Figure 1).

She decorates the wool with spirals of lightly palmed wool strips and yarn, dots of wool, and teased-open mohair locks. To secure them to the surface of the scarf, she pokes them with a fine felting needle, working on a foam surface, before she tops them with wisps of wool. To 2 qt (1.9 l) of room temperature water, Elizabeth adds ½ tsp (2.5 ml) of Dr. Bronner's Lavender soap. (Always add the soap to the water, rather than the water to the soap.)

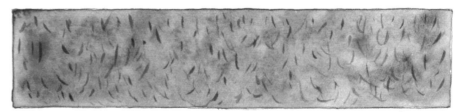

Figure 1. Arrange wool on the silk fabric

Elizabeth uses a nylon sheer curtain to cover the work. Imagining the scarf divided into thirds, she works one-third at a time. Sprinkling the third being worked with about one-third of the soapy water, she presses down on the sheer curtain and spreads the water out to the edges of the scarf. Unlike when using a plastic sheet, water can be added to the work through the sheer curtain. When this third is thoroughly wet, she wets the middle and then the last third.

Felt wool into silk

Holding the sheer curtain in place, Elizabeth begins rubbing it with a juice reamer, a highly textured pestle she found in the gadget aisle of the supermarket. She takes her time, rubbing the entire surface in big circular motions and spending 15 minutes or more. Occasionally she lifts the sheer curtain to prevent it from attaching to the wool and to check the felting process.

Elizabeth rolls up the bubble wrap, scarf, and sheer around the pipe insulation and secures it with the nylon stockings and felts using the rolling method. She counts every back and forth as she works. After every 100 she unties the bundle and examines the scarf's underside for fibers that have migrated through the base fabric. Until they do, she resumes rolling.

Full the scarf

To full the felted scarf, Elizabeth folds the scarf to fit within the large ziplock bag. After squeezing out the air, she throws the package straight down onto the floor, table, or bathtub, with as much force as she can muster. Impact propels the wool fibers into the weave of the silk. The package must hit the surface straight on; if the contents are splayed outward, the wool is pulled out of the fabric. After a few slams, she examines the scarf for the ruches and puckers that signal her success.

Elizabeth squeezes the scarf under hot running water, then cold water, then hot water again. She rolls it vigorously against the bubble surface of the bubble wrap for added results. Any spots of wool that have not felted into the silk can be coaxed through by rubbing the silk underside with a rubber glove.

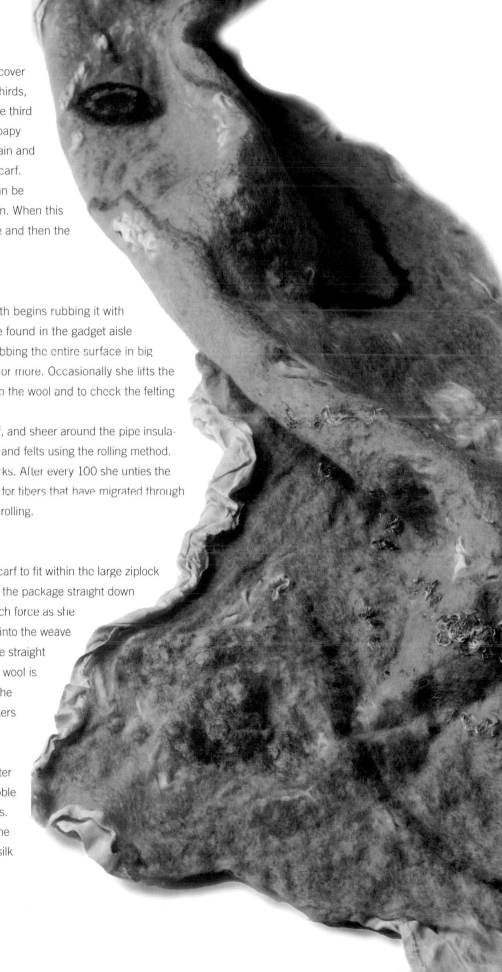

Ulonga-Bora Tote Bag

About the Artist

ALEXA GINSBURG refers to her first feltmaking experiences as a "chance encounter with roving and warm soapy water," which provided the impetus to study the form further. She was hooked by the sensation of the wool in her hands, the diverse and complex play of color and the range of possible shapes, forms, and patterns that handfelting offers. Hand-dyeing her own silk fabrics to incorporate in her feltmaking heightens the creative adventure for her.

Alexa Ginsburg is intrigued by the complex cloth achieved by felting into silk. She frequently incorporates handdyed or printed silk fabric in her feltmaking, not simply as the base fabric, but also as surface decoration, providing added color and texture. Though weightless and supple, this felt is deceptively strong and perfect for her handbags and totes.

She named this bag for the fictional river in the movie *African Queen*. She chose bold, primitive lines executed in dark earth tones to reflect the jungle's mystery and inlaid handdyed silk to convey lush vegetation illuminated by patches of golden light. This sophisticated bag, lined with silk for extra strength, is lightweight enough to carry to Ulonga-Bora or any destination.

Key Techniques

- *Make a clear vinyl resist*
- *Snip and rip fabric*
- *Dye silk*
- *Felt in three dimensions*
- *Make Nuno felt*
- *Create surface design with inlaid silk fabric*

Materials

- 4½ oz (135 g) solid-colored merino divided among several colors
- 1 yd (91.5 cm) Habotoi 5 mm silk, 44" (112 cm) wide
- Upholstery thread

In Alexa's Studio

- 5 gal (19 l) fertilizer sprayer
- 20 × 24" (51 × 61 cm) clear upholstery vinyl
- Permanent marker
- Scissors
- Ruler
- 20 × 25" (51 × 63.5 cm) plastic sheet
- 2 plastic sandwich bags
- 30 × 40" (76 × 101.5 cm) solar pool cover
- 20 × 25" (51 × 63.5 cm) fiberglass replacement window screen
- 3 ties made from pantyhose
- Towels
- Sewing needle
- Olive oil bar soap
- Pair of plastic gloves or 2 sandwich baggies
- Rubber gloves
- Pool noodle
- Ridged mat
- Sushi mat
- Iron
- Fiber Reactive Procion MX dye
- Soda ash
- Salt
- 8 oz (240 ml) or larger plastic cup
- 2 bowls, one large enough to contain the other
- Microwave oven

Finished measurements

Bag: 16" (40.5 cm) tall and 13" (33 cm) wide
Handles: 19" (48.5 cm)

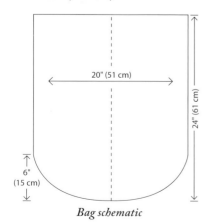

20" (51 cm)

24" (61 cm)

6" (15 cm)

Bag schematic

Make a resist

Alexa marks the midpoint of one 20" (51 cm) edge of the upholstery vinyl, which will be the bottom edge, and 6" up one 24" (61 cm) edge, which will be one side (see bag resist schematic below). She softens the corner by drawing an arc between the marks. By folding the vinyl in half and cutting along the arc, she makes a symmetrical resist.

Snip and rip the silk

As Elizabeth Buchtman does (see page 72), Alexa launders the silk before dyeing it. On a 36" (91.5 cm) edge of the silk, Alexa makes a snip 11" (28 cm) from the corner and rips an 11 x 44" (28 x 112 cm) strip of silk. Snipping the center of an 11" (28 cm) edge, she rips it again into two 5½ x 44" (14 x 112 cm) pieces, from which she snips and rips 16 squares, 5½" (14 cm) each side.

Snipping the midpoint of the 44" (112 cm) edge of the 25" (63.5 cm) piece of silk, she rips it into 2 identical 22 x 25" (56 x 63.5 cm) rectangles (larger than the resist).

The snip-and-rip technique is quick, satisfying, downright cathartic, and it also provides straight and square results. The frayed edges work into the wool in a most appealing way.

Dye silk

Wearing gloves to prevent dyeing her hands, Alexa stirs ¼ tsp (1.5 ml) Fiber Reactive Procion MX dye, ½ tsp (2.5 ml) soda ash, and ½ tsp (2.5 ml) salt into a plastic cup containing 1 cup (240 ml) warm water. To create a mottled effect, she bunches each piece of silk and loosely binds it with a rubber band before dunking it in the dye. She places each dyed piece of silk in a plastic bag. She pours 1" (2.5 cm) of water into the larger bowl, then settles the smaller bowl inside it (like a double boiler or the water bath employed in baking custard). She places the plastic bagged silk pieces in the small bowl. After heating the bag-filled bowls in the microwave oven on medium setting for 2 minutes, she opens the bags and allows steam to escape, then microwaves them for 2 more minutes. She allows the silk to cure for 12 hours before rinsing until water runs clear.

Create three-dimensional Nuno felt

Alexa cuts both of the 22 x 25" (56 x 63.5 cm) pieces of silk, one to the exact size of the resist, and the other ½" (1.3 cm) larger than the pattern all around the edge except the straight 20" (50 cm) edge, which will become the opening.

First side

Alexa covers the resist with the larger piece of silk, allowing it to extend beyond all but the straight top edge. She places thin wisps of roving along and 1" (2.5 cm) beyond the silk's edges (Figure 1). She builds no fewer than 8 extremely thin perpendicular layers of fiber. Thinner and more numerous layers provide greater opportunities for the fibers to tangle and knot as they move among each other.

She saturates the wool with soapy water, tops it with fiberglass replacement window screening, and rubs it all over. If the wool is not thoroughly wet, she adds more water through the screening. She prefers screening to a sheet of plastic because lifting plastic could disturb the wool, posing a threat to the design and compromising the felting process. To avoid pulling wool up through the screening, Alexa wears the plastic gloves or liberally soaps her hands. She presses a cellulose sponge against the screen to absorb some water, making it much more manageable to flip the work over. After rubbing for a few minutes, she carefully replaces the screening with a sheet of plastic, then flips the piece over.

Second side

Alexa pats the vinyl resist dry and folds just the edges of the first piece of silk up over the edge of the resist. She places the second piece of silk on top, covering the turned edges, before folding the wool from the first side over the edges of the resist and onto the top piece of silk. She places thin wisps of roving along and 1" (2.5 cm) beyond the silk's edges, a repeat of side one. She wets and rubs this side for a few minutes before flipping the resist over and then folding up the wool that extends beyond the edge.

Inlay silk fabric for surface design

Alexa decorates the wet wool with the silk squares, folding a few over the edge of the seamless join (Figure 2). She occasionally decorates the silk squares, or the wool between them, with roving in thin strips or little dots formed like loose spitballs.

Felt and full the bag

Alexa lifts up the entire work and places it on the smooth side of the solar cover, then covers it with plastic. She rolls it up on the pool noodle, secures it with the pantyhose legs tied in a loop knot that is easily untied, then uses the rolling method to felt it until it passes the pinch test.

She fulls the bag by gently rubbing the silk portions against a ridged mat or the bubble side of the solar cover. She rolls up the bag and kneads it along the ridges or bubbles, rerolling it from each edge to work it evenly. Cutting the top edge of the bag, she removes the resist, then rubs the cut edges against the ridged mat to toughen it.

When she is nearly finished felting and fulling the bag, Alexa draws additional fibers through the silk interior by rubbing it gently in small circles with a rubber-gloved hand. She resumes kneading it against the textured surface until it reduces to two-thirds of the original size.

Make felt handles

Alexa splits one 16" (40.5 cm) length of roving in half lengthwise. She snips and rips strips of silk, then wraps each end of the roving with a piece of silk and wisps of roving (Figure 3). She rubs the 2 strips of roving against the ridged mat, then wets and rolls them until they are firm and solid. She pins the handles to the top of the tote and sews them in place with upholstery thread.

Fertilizer sprayer

Once she has filled the sprayer with water and a few squirts of dishwashing liquid, Alexa has room temperature water whenever she needs it. She favors spray to dispense water to the wool, and this equipment makes it easy to control the amount and flow of water. It is especially convenient for working in a space that has no running water.

Plastic disposable gloves

The one-time-use plastic gloves packaged with hair color and home permanents or commonly used by food-handlers are dandy for handling the developing felt without disturbing the fiber. If you lack a pair, slip each hand in a sandwich baggie.

Figure 1. Cover the resist with roving

Figure 2. Place the silk square surface decorations

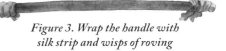

Figure 3. Wrap the handle with silk strip and wisps of roving

Transfixed Butterfly Cape

About the Artist

 LUCY ZERCHER has been a weaver, spinner, and knitter since 1989, so it was only a matter of time before she became a felter. Her extensive travels are reflected in her work, and her pieces are displayed in juried exhibitions and galleries abroad, in Alaska and throughout the United States, as well as in museums in Budapest and Alaska. A special education teacher with a focus on blindness, she demonstrates, lectures, and teaches feltmaking upon request.

Lucy Zercher was a knitter and weaver when she came upon feltmaking in 1989. Felt offers the combination of painterly possibilities; the ability to create bold forms and light drapable fabrics; and the flexibility to integrate other materials.

Within her daily routine, Lucy often pauses to observe common things for their pleasing color composition, unusual form, or interesting texture. She files them in her head to retrieve at another time and interpret in felt. Her work starts as a recollection, a memory that takes form as a mental image. With warm soapy water and soft fibers, she creates the image in tangible form. "Transfixed" recalls a hike in the Monarch butterfly sanctuary around Rosario, Mexico, when butterflies landed on her, sometimes by the dozens. The cape's patterned body extends out from a bug-like form on the front that serves as the closure.

Key Techniques

- *Design a pattern with contrasting removable templates*
- *Create three-dimensional hollow sculpture*

Materials

- 10 oz (300 g) solid-colored merino wool roving, half in main color, the rest divided among 4 accent colors
- 2 yd (183 cm) Habotoi 5 mm silk
- Sewing thread
- 2 metal sew-on snaps

In Lucy's Studio

- Scissors
- White paper
- 77" (196.5 cm) square black plastic
- 8' (244 cm) square bubble wrap (regular clear variety, not solar cover)
- 11 × 16" (28 × 40.5 cm) sheet closed-cell foam (thin, dense foam packing sheet)
- 8' (244 cm) square mosquito netting
- 2" (5 cm) diameter PVC pipe
- Sewing needle
- Velcro straps
- Ridged rubber mat
- 36-gauge felting needle
- Stiff toothbrush
- Scotch tape
- Permanent marker
- Olive oil soap

Finished measurements

44" (112 cm) diameter

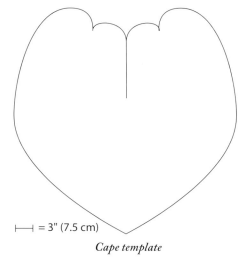

⊢—⊣ = 3" (7.5 cm)

Cape template

Design a pattern with contrasting removable templates

Each of Lucy's garment designs begins with a color sketch, in which she anticipates the shapes of the inlaid fabric design. She renders a mockup in muslin (as a tailor would do) to exact dimensions with the designs outlined before committing it to wool and silk.

Lucy first draws the outline of the cape on black plastic at about double the size of the finished cape (see cape template below). She draws silhouettes of the design's shapes on white paper at nearly twice the size of the desired finished pieces, then cuts them out. Arranging the cutout shapes on the black plastic, Lucy cuts out a black plastic pattern about 6½' (198 cm) square, which will produce a finished cape about 3' (106.5 cm) square (Figure 1).

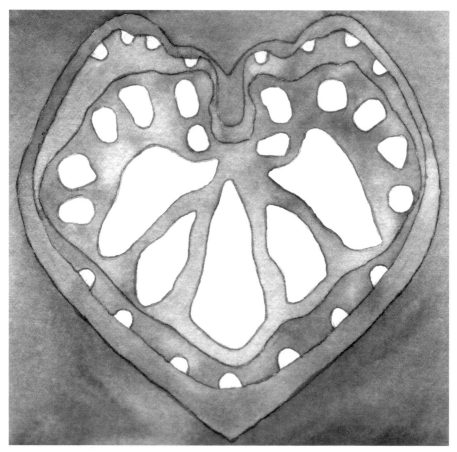

Figure 1. Arrange cutout shapes on black plastic pattern

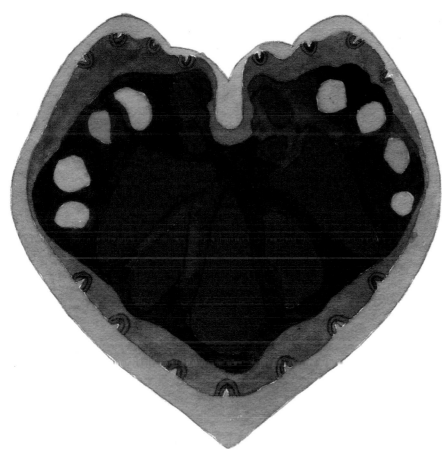

Figure 2. Place silk and roving

Place fabric and fiber using the pattern

One at a time, Lucy lifts each white paper shape and uses it as a template for cutting out a silk fabric shape. She then returns each piece of paper to its place on the black plastic, taping it down.

Lucy uses the black plastic as a pattern or "cartoon" (a template used in weaving) to precisely arrange the fiber for her design. She places the bubble wrap smooth-side up on the black plastic pattern (Figure 1).

The right side of the cape will develop facedown against the bubble wrap. Lucy places each silk shape on the bubble wrap, matching it to the corresponding shape on the pattern. Reserving some of the roving for the closure and referring to the sketch of the cape regularly, she places 2 thin perpendicular layers of colored merino fiber (Figure 2). When she is satisfied with the arrangement of the fiber and silk, Lucy felts the cape by covering it with mosquito netting, rolling the bubble wrap/silk/wool/netting layers up on the PVC pipe, securing it with Velcro straps, and using the rolling method. She fulls it by tossing and kneading it until it matches the original mockup (as in Elizabeth's scarf on page 71).

Swatching

Familiar with the idea of swatching from her experience as a knitter, Lucy learned to felt a sample square of the selected fiber to determine the thickness of the layers needed for the desired drape and the percentage of shrinkage. Many of Lucy's wearables are made of 2 thin layers which, like this cape, shrink by about 50%.

Create insect closure

Lucy builds a three-dimensional hollow sculpture in the shape of an insect for the cape's closure.

Insect body

Lucy draws an insect to the desired finished size. She then draws it twice as large on the closed-cell foam and cuts it out to produce the resist. She wraps the resist with 4–6 thin layers of less than 1 oz (30 g) of fiber, then covers this with mosquito netting.

She wets and rubs the wool, working toward the interior and being careful not to spread or thin the fiber at the edges. When the fibers on one side start to firm, she flips it over and works the other side. (This is small version of the felting around a resist method used for the boots, beret, and slippers on pages 46, 52, 64).

Antennae

Lucy lays out an 8" (20 cm) length of roving. Leaving the ends dry and wetting only the center, Lucy rolls it back and forth against the bubble side of bubble wrap as though making a clay snake. When it is firm and solid, she cuts the piece in half diagonally, palming and tapering the cut ends. She uses the toothbrush to loosen some fibers on the insect head where she'll place the antennae. Placing the dry ends of both antennae there, she first needle-felts them into place and then wet-felts them until they are attached (Figure 3).

Full and shape the bug

When it is felted, she makes a slit to remove the resist, then begins to knead the bug, at first gently, building to vigorously, to full it. Every few minutes she heats it in steam or hot water and alternates between pinching the appendages accordion-like and pulling them as though extending a telescope. She continues to full until it shrinks to 6" (15 cm) long.

Allowing the front of the cape to overlap slightly, she sews a snap closure into place, then sews the insect onto the cape's overlap.

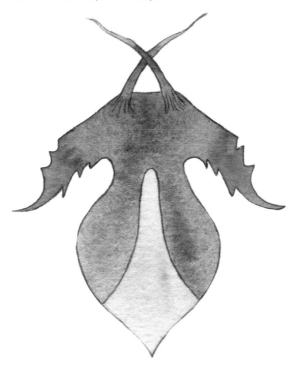

Figure 3. Place the dry antennae ends on the insect head

Tea Dress

About the Artist
CAROL HUBER CYPHER felted around a ball with Beth Beede (page 10) many years ago, sealing her fate as feltmaker. Formerly a professional chef, she so enjoyed over a decade of teaching at fiber conferences and fiber stores whenever her schedule permitted that she hung up her toque in 2001 to teach, felt, bead, and write full time. She is the author of two previous books, and her work is published in books and magazines internationally. Carol teaches feltmaking, beadwork, and the provocative pairing of the two nationwide. She has appeared on television shows for PBS and DIY networks. She teaches a course in the fashion program at Marist College.

Carol Huber Cypher enjoys imagining her surroundings rendered in felt: the elephant ear leaf in an ornamental garden transformed into fine merino felt, clouds reflected on the lake evoked in merino and bombyx silk felt; a traffic light viewed through a rain-spattered windshield rendered in beaded felt. No other medium has offered her felt's capacity for color and shape. Having explored nearly every form of fiber work, Carol finds the most appeal from "scrumbling" (free-form crochet), spinning, beadwork, and feltmaking. Every aspect of these forms is colorful, engaging, meditative, and sensuous, and each presents the opportunity for creative expression.

Imagine beginning a morning with white gauze, wool, water, and magic, and finishing that afternoon with a tea dress, in your color, shape, style, and exact size, without a single stitch.

Key Techniques

- *Create layered surface design with a skewer*
- *Create stitchless joins*
- *Shape a waistline without darts*
- *Stain with tea*

Materials
- 36 × 132" (91.5 × 335 cm) cotton gauze fabric
- 4 oz (120 g) solid-colored merino, divided among 4 colors
- 10 teabags

In Carol's Studio
- 48 × 72" (122 × 183 cm) solar pool cover
- 48 × 72" (122 × 183 cm) plastic sheet
- Paper plate
- 36 × 72" (91.5 × 183 cm) plastic sheet
- 48" (122 cm) pipe insulation
- 3 nylon ties made from pantyhose legs
- Skewer
- Scissors
- Permanent marker
- Towels
- 2 plastic supermarket bags
- Castile soap scented with essential oils

Finished measurements
47" (119.5 cm) long; 32" (81.5 cm) wide.

Prepare the dress fabric

Carol folds the fabric in half widthwise. She lays the solar pool cover on a table with the bubble-side down, then smooths the doubled fabric flat on top of it. She lifts the top layer of fabric and allows it to fall off the table.

She folds the paper plate in half, then folds it again, lengthwise (not into quadrants). She unfolds it and cuts along any fold except the centerfold. She aligns the cut edge with the fold in the fabric, traces the plate, and cuts the paper plate outline out of the fabric (Figure 1). This is the front of the dress. She replaces the cut edge of the plate on the fabric fold line, this time on the back of the dress, and traces and cuts out the back neckline.

Decorate the dress front

Carol splits the roving into long strips and decorates the fabric with long vertical pieces, then places wisps of roving along the hemline, neckline, and top 12" (30.5 cm) of each side where the armhole will be (Figure 2).

Because the wool only serves as surface design on the dress front fabric, Carol decorates without regard for layering and crossing fiber. In addition to long strips of roving and wisps that resemble brush strokes, she decorates with concentric circles or ovals made by layering wool on a skewer (see Skewer Maneuver, page 87).

Having applied all the desired wool surface design, Carol dribbles cool soapy water on the surface, covers it with plastic sheeting, and rubs it, smoothing the wool to the edge of the fabric. The wool will wrap around the edge of the fabric, concealing jagged or frayed edges.

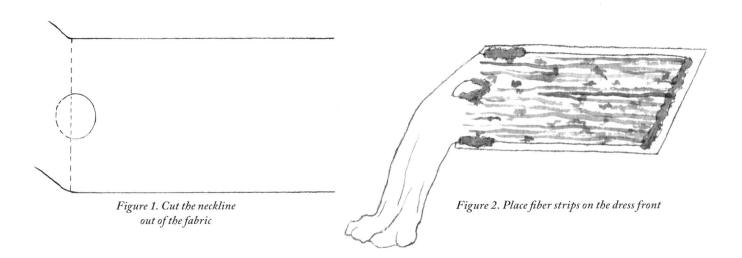

Figure 1. Cut the neckline out of the fabric

Figure 2. Place fiber strips on the dress front

Prepare the dress back

Carol rolls up the plastic-covered fabric and wool (without the solar cover) onto the pipe insulation (Figure 3). She pulls the rolled up section to the edge of the table, placing the entire back of the dress on the solar cover. After decorating, wetting, and rubbing this section through plastic sheeting as she did the front, she rolls the bundle forward to wind the back of the dress onto the roll.

Arrange resists inside dress

Carol lays the plastic resist out on the solar cover and, rotating the roll 180 degrees, places it on the resist 12" (30.5 cm) from the end. She unrolls the plastic-covered back of the dress onto the resist. Carefully, she flips the resist, dress back, and plastic sheet "sandwich" over onto the smooth side of the solar cover. To prevent the armholes from felting closed, she places a plastic bag on each side at the armhole area (Figure 4).

Bringing the rolled-up material up over the resist, she unrolls the plastic sheet-covered front onto the resist.

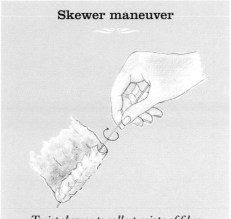

Skewer maneuver

Twist skewer to roll up wisps of fiber

Carol covers a 4" (10 cm) square area with wisps of wool in a single color. Laying the skewer across the wool 1" (2.5 cm) from one edge, she brushes the tips of the fiber back over the skewer and begins rolling the skewer between thumb and forefinger in one direction only until the fiber grabs onto it.

Once all of the fiber has collected on the skewer like cotton candy, she covers a 4 × 6" (10 × 15 cm) area with a second color of fiber. Using the same fiber-coated skewer, she repeats the process, layering three or four colors this way before sliding the wool "cigar" off the skewer. She cuts the piece diagonally every ½" (1.3 cm) to produce feather or eye medallions that make beautiful surface design.

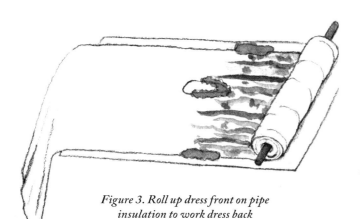

Figure 3. Roll up dress front on pipe insulation to work dress back

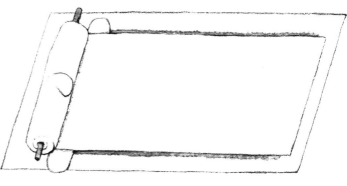

Figure 4. Arrange resists between dress front and back

Seamless sides

Carol places wool along and beyond the back edges to bring up over the front, filling in any thin areas (Figure 5). This fiber will join the dress front and back seamlessly and without sewing.

After wrapping the wool over the edges to seamlessly join the dress-front and back, she felts the work by rolling it up on the pipe insulation, securing it with the nylon ties, and rolling it back and forth until wool migrates through the gauze as shown in the photograph at left.

Shape the waistline without darts

Carol examines the dress and fulls it to nearly the finished size. Gathering the dress at the waistline, she rolls the area along the bubble side of the solar cover, dunks it in hot soapy water, and rolls some more. She palms it between her pressed-together hands to shrink the fabric widthwise (Figure 6).

Stain with tea

To impart a soft tint and take the glare off the white cloth, Carol soaks the dress for 20 minutes in 1 gal (3.8 l) hot water with 10 teabags and ½ cup (120 ml) vinegar

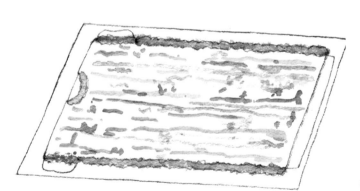

Figure 5. Place wool for seamless join

Figure 6. Full waistline

Inside of dress

Zebrine Vest

About the Artist
CASSIE LEWIS earned a masters degree in educational leadership from William Patterson University in New Jersey during her career as a public school teacher, and she continued graduate studies there in textile design and fiber arts. Workshops in a variety of fiber techniques fueled her growing fascination. She enjoys teaching feltmaking in her Warwick, New York, studio; Sugar Maples Center for Arts and Education in Hunter, New York; and the Newark Museum, Newark, New Jersey.

Cassie Lewis is intrigued by the idea of creating fabric in this twenty-first century with the same simplistic methods used by the ancients. She finds the manual work physically and mentally satisfying.

Over a decade ago, in Cassie's very first feltmaking class, Beth Beede taught her this technique for constructing a vest. To make a very lightweight yet strong garment, the fibers are carefully arranged in thin crossed layers. Admiring similar surface design in other fabric, she developed a technique to re-create it in her felt. Within the multiple thin layers of wool, she adds thin wisps of black to specific areas to yield dark stripes that blend into the background.

Key Techniques

- *Make a vest pattern*
- *Use a resist to overlap the front*
- *Join the sides seamlessly*

Materials

- 3½ oz (105 g) solid-colored merino in main color
- 1 oz (30 g) each solid-colored merino in three accent colors
- ¼ oz (7.5 g) black merino
- Liquid soap
- Water

In Cassie's Studio

- 36 × 72" (91.5 × 183 cm) craft paper
- 28" (71 cm) square or larger plastic
- 36 × 72" (91.5 × 183 cm) or larger bubble wrap
- 36 × 72" (91.5 × 183 cm) or larger plastic sheet
- 10 gallon-size plastic bags
- 36" (91.5 cm) long 1" (2.5 cm) diameter dowel
- 3 ties made from pantyhose legs
- Nylon or polyester sheer curtain
- Needle and thread
- Straight pins
- Permanent marker
- Scissors

Finished measurements

About 43" (109 cm) chest circumference and 21" (53.5 cm) long.

Make a vest pattern

Cassie uses the entire piece of craft paper to sketch a vest pattern as one piece from back to front, leaving it open at the side seams. Knowing how readily it expands, she makes the neck opening small. After cutting out the pattern, she traces it onto the smooth side of the bubble wrap. (She stores the paper pattern for future use.)

Cut resists

From the plastic sheeting, Cassie cuts a 7" (18 cm) square resist for the pocket and an 18 x 28" (45.5 x 71 cm) rectangle resist for the overlapped front opening. She draws a line lengthwise down the center of the rectangle.

Divide the wool into portions

Cassie divides the roving into 10 equal portions and places each portion in a bag. She will build only 2 thin perpendicular layers of the vest on each of 5 sections: back right; front right; back left; front left; and front overlap resist, pocket resist, and optional collar.

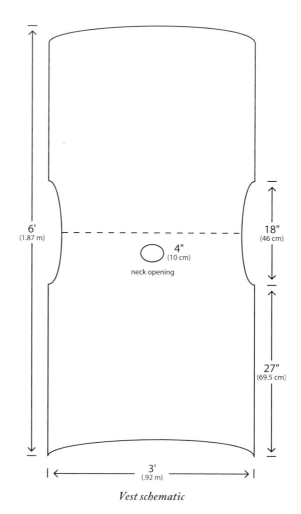

6'
(1.87 m)

18"
(46 cm)

4"
(10 cm)

neck opening

27"
(69.5 cm)

3'
(.92 m)

Vest schematic

Place the first layer of fiber

Cassie lays the contents of one bag of fiber in a thin, even layer of roving across the back right (section 3), then does the same to cover the front right (section 4) with one bag and the back left (section 1) with one bag. She places one-third of the fiber in the next bag on the front (section 2), extending the wisps of fiber 9" (23 cm) past the center line that separates the front right from front left (Figure 1).

Place the front resist

She centers the 18 x 28" (45.5 x 71 cm) resist on the front. From a full bag of fiber, she lays one-third in a thin, even layer of wisps across the front right of the vest, working on top of the resist where it overlaps the front left. She lays another third of the unfinished bag, extending 9" (23 cm) past the center line that separates front right from front left. She avoids extending wisps beyond the resist's edges to prevent the two layers from felting closed (Figure 2). She reserves the remaining third of this bag to lay across the pocket resist, extending 1" (2.5 cm) past three of its four edges.

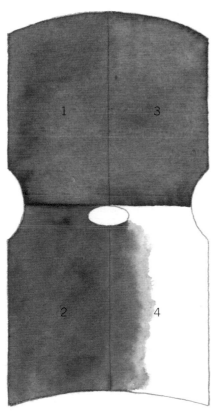

Figure 1. Place the first layer of fiber

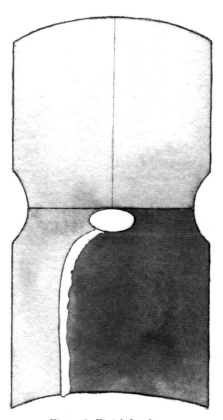

Figure 2. Finish first layer

Place the second layer of fiber

Cassie uses the remaining 5 bags in the same fashion, placing thin wisps evenly across and perpendicular to the layers created by the first 5 bags. She lifts the far edge of the front resist to place wisps on the part that extends past the front right and puts it back down to extend beyond the front left.

Cassie places the pocket on the front of the vest with the wool extending beyond the side and bottom edges, so the top of the pocket is open (Figure 3). She partially felts the collar and vest separately before basting them together to felt seamlessly.

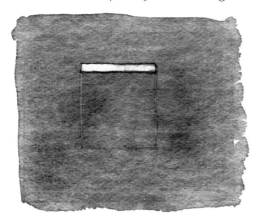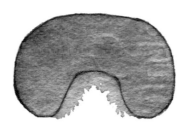

Figure 3. Place roving over pocket and collar

Felt and join the vest

To wet the area beneath the resist, she carefully lifts the front resist, dribbles hot soapy water on the wool, and settles the front resist back down. Cassie felts the vest halfway before joining the front and back seamlessly. Successful joins of partially felted pieces rely on the work being felted enough to hold together but not felted enough to resist the other felt.

She folds the plastic sheet in half to use as a resist between the front and back of the vest. She lifts up two corners at the hem and folds the work onto the resist, joining the side seams with the front over the back. She pins the overlapped sides together from the underarms to the center to the bottom edge. She bastes them together with large running stitches in contrasting thread that will be removed later, then removes the pins (Figure 4).

Holding one hand inside and one outside the piece, she rubs the joins until they are felted together seamlessly. She joins the collar to the neckline in the same way. She then fulls the vest to the desired finished size.

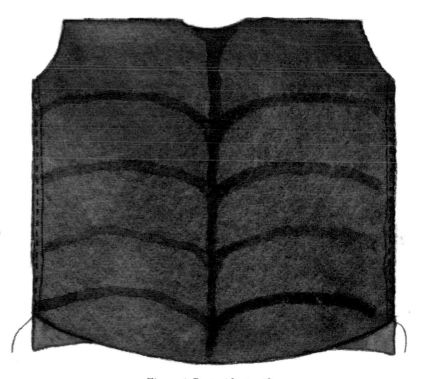

Figure 4. Baste sides together

Floating Poppies

About the Artist
LINDA BROOKS HIRSCHMAN
enjoyed precious little time for her fiber
art while balancing a career as a systems
analyst and technical writer with the
demands of marriage and raising two
children. After a bout with meningitis
and departing from the business world
fifteen years ago, she became a studio
fiber artist. She enjoys constructing
her own cloth and manipulating it for
dramatic texture. Working intuitively, she
combines feltmaking, hand and machine
sewing, beadwork, and basketry in her
sculptures. Her work is held in corporate
and private collections and displayed in
magazines and galleries.

Linda Brooks Hirschman, inspired by the brilliant color and
unique flower-like shapes of Dale Chihuly's glass sculptures,
wondered if she could transform her handmade felt into a three-
dimensional translucent sculpture that resembles glass.

Her hanging installation is a series of felt poppies, a joyous field
of vibrant flowers where no two are the same size, shape, or design.
The poppies are light enough to sway in a breeze and retain their
shape despite being suspended by their center. Viewed from below,
they appear illuminated. Linda achieved these results by combining
her favorite fiber techniques, feltmaking and handsewing.

Key Techniques

- *Lay out fibers for circular felt*
- *Use a vibrating sander*
- *Wrap and sew a wire rim*
- *Stiffen the center with polyurethane*

Materials

For each poppy:
- 3.5 oz (105 g) solid-colored merino, divided among 4 colors
- 1 eye from a hook-and-eye set
- 3 yd (274.5 cm) lengths of various yarns (bouclé, eyelash, chenille, variegated, slubby, worsted)

For entire piece:
- Spool of sewing thread to match yarn
- 80" (203 cm) stainless steel 19-gauge wire
- Fast-drying oil-based polyurethane

In Linda's Studio
- 30" (76 cm) firm plastic for pattern
- 30" (76 cm) square bubble wrap
- Thin lightweight plastic, such as a dry cleaner bag
- Permanent marker
- Castile soap
- Coin to use as a marker
- Ruler or measuring tape
- Bristle paint brush
- Vibrating sander
- 12" (30.5 cm) diameter Styrofoam ball or rounded bowl
- Sewing needle
- Scissors
- Steamer or kettle
- Straight pins

Finished measurements
The poppies vary in width and size. Poppies shown measure 15–20" (38–51 cm) in diameter.

Lay out fiber for circular felt

Linda draws a 24" (61 cm) diameter circle drawn with a permanent marker on firm plastic. She draws 2 smaller concentric circles indicating the separation between the bands of color and marks the center with an X. She places the bubble wrap bubble side down onto the pattern. She divides each of the 3 colors of roving in half, reserving one-half for each layer.

Starting with the color band at the edge, she lays even and overlapping wisps of roving with all fibers parallel along the 24" (61 cm) diameter circle (Figure 1). Once she has completed the first round, she makes another pass, laying a ring of wisps just inside and overlapping those in place. She lays additional smaller rounds, changing color as indicated in the pattern, until the entire pattern is covered in 3 bands of color (Figure 2).

This layer, the "outside," is the top of the poppy and will face the ceiling when it hangs. She lays a coin on the area marked X, marking it temporarily.

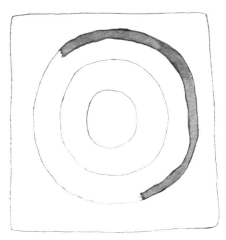

Figure 1. Lay parallel fibers along the edge

Figure 2. Cover the circles with 3 bands of color

Place a second layer

Linda places a second layer of roving on top of and perpendicular to the first layer, this time radiating from the center like the hands of a clock (Figure 3). Starting with the border color, she covers the concentric wisps of the border color with radial wisps of the same color. She covers all 3 bands in this way.

Radial wisps allow a bit of one color to overlap another. Adjusting the width of the overlapping wisps gives Linda control over the amount of bleeding between the bands of color. Layering two different colors within a band will blend them. For example, she can achieve a range of oranges by layering yellow and red, or she can eliminate blending by maintaining crisp, clearly defined edges between the color bands.

Linda places the coin at the center on top of this layer. Before wetting and felting the piece, she examines the fiber for uniformity, as thin spots and holes will become more evident with light passing through them.

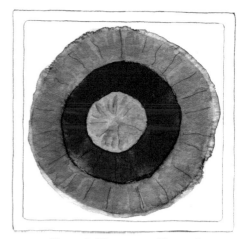

Figure 3. Place a second layer of roving radiating from the center

Wet and embellish the flower

Linda sprinkles the wool with cool, soapy water, then covers it with plastic and rubs the wool toward the center, being sure to maintain a firm edge. She removes the plastic and decorates the flower with the yarn, using contrasting colors to create petals, lines, loops, or other shapes. When she is satisfied with the decoration, she covers the piece with plastic and presses the yarn into the flower.

Felt with a vibrating sander

After wetting the wool, Linda checks that the electric sander is grounded. She starts by pressing the sander lightly into the design, peeking at the design regularly until all the fibers are locked into place. She then lightly "sands" the entire circle.

Linda has learned not to become too attached to the design; as she says, "Shift happens!" Holding the piece up to the light, she checks for holes, then flips the piece over. She repairs any holes or thin spots by adding roving to this side. She "sands" this side until it is softly felted. When she has finished with the sander, Linda fulls the piece against the bubble side of the bubble wrap.

Shape and dry the piece

Linda drapes the piece over a Styrofoam ball or bowl, stretching the edges slightly and molding the center over the round shape. She allows it to dry and then irons it. If the edges are jagged or thin, she trims them with scissors.

Felting with a power tool?

A vibrating sander jiggles fibers into each other, promoting felting. Some feltmakers create entire wall hangings with the tool. Some felt artists, concerned about combining an electric appliance with water, use a cordless version and a plastic barrier to separate wet wool from a power tool. Linda is much more nonchalant about it—she just plunges a grounded sander into wet wool. For safety reasons, you may skip the sander all together and simply felt the piece by rolling it in the bubble wrap.

Attach wire rim

Linda cuts the wire a few inches longer than the circumference of the poppy and wraps it with a yarn that contrasts with the border color. She ties the yarn to one end of the wire, wraps the entire wire, and ties off the yarn.

Wanting the stitches to show in the poppy's edge, Linda threads a sewing needle with thread the same color as the wrapping yarn. Starting 2" (5 cm) from one end of the wire, she handsews the wrapped wire to the edge of the poppy, pulling the thread snug and keeping the stitches close together. When the ends meet, she overlaps them no more than 1" (2.5 cm). She cuts off the extra wire and winds the remaining yarn around the overlapped wires, sewing the ends together.

Stiffen the center

After researching and experimenting extensively with stiffeners, Linda prefers to use oil-based polyurethane; its odor lingers for a while and mineral spirits are required to clean the brush, but it takes only two layers to become rock-hard.

She sews the eye to the back center of the poppy. She drapes the poppy over the Styrofoam ball or bowl again with the designed side down. She paints a thin layer of polyurethane in a 4" (10 cm) circle around the eye to produce the dome of the piece. The polyurethane should sit on the surface of the felt, not leak through to the other side. (If she has not rinsed the felt well enough, it will be absorbent.) When the first coat is dry, Linda paints another coat or two. The finished poppy should be firm to maintain a domed rather than peaked center when hanging.

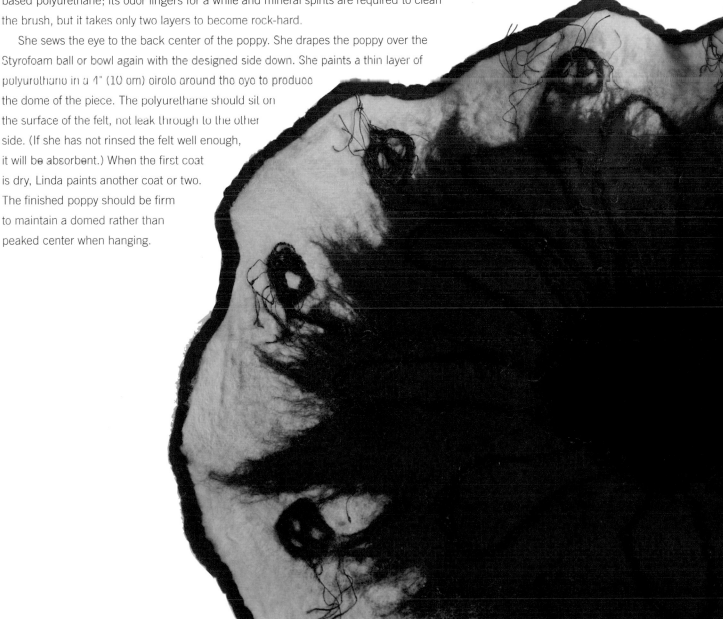

Cascading Collar

About the Artist
GAR WANG studied sculpture at
Princeton University and in graduate
school at Hunter College. She taught
drawing and painting at both Princeton
University and Hunter College and
received a National Endowment for
the Arts grant in painting. Her friend
Cassie Lewis (page 90) introduced her to
feltmaking, opening a whole new world
of possibilities.

Gar Wang, a painter and sculptor, enjoys feltmaking as an organic
process that enables color and shape to evolve simultaneously.
She was attracted to felting for its ancient origins, use of raw and
readily available material, and rudimentary process. She describes
her work as spontaneous and intuitive and finds feltmaking
refreshingly direct and wholesome.

Gar begins her neckpiece, a marriage of scarf and collar, by
layering the fiber with concern for color composition. There are no
straight edges here—the contours of the outline foretell what is to
come. A second smaller layer, connected by the deliberate placement of resists and denser where it joins, will be stretched and
rolled into high-profile ruffles and frills.

Key Techniques

- *Use resists to create ruffles*
- *Roll and stretch ruffles*

Materials

- 1½ oz (45 g) each of two main colors of solid-colored merino
- ½ oz (45 g) each of 5 accent colors of solid-colored merino

In Gar's Studio

- 3 × 7' (91.5 x 213.5 cm) bubble wrap
- 3 × 7' (91.5 x 213.5 cm) plastic sheets
- Plastic bag
- Fiberglass window replacement screen
- Scissors
- Towel
- Marker
- Ivory liquid soap

Finished measurements

37" (94 cm) long; 13" (33 cm) wide; 13" (33 cm) collar; 7 × 9" (18 × 23 cm) neck opening; 24" (61 cm) length (one ruffle); 18" (45.5 cm) length (second ruffle).

Lay out fiber for scarf

Gar begins by drawing a wavy outline for the scarf on the smooth side of the bubble wrap with a permanent marker. She places about one-third of the roving in three perpendicular layers over the sketch, varying the colors to please her eye (Figure 1). When she is satisfied with the arrangement, she sprinkles the fiber with hot soapy water and covers with the screen. She rubs with a crumpled plastic bag, then removes the screen.

Place resists and fiber for collar

Gar places a plastic sheet over the top portion of the scarf from about halfway down the piece to 1" (2.5 cm) from the edge of the fiber. She draws on the plastic a wavy shape with an oval opening at its center large enough to slip over the head (Figure 2). She places about one-fourth of the remaining wool in 3 perpendicular layers on top of the sketch, allowing the fiber to extend into the opening by 1" (2.5 cm). She wets this area with hot soapy water, covers it with the screen, and rubs with a plastic bag.

Place resists and fiber for neck ruffle

Gar cuts an oval-shaped hole from another piece of plastic that corresponds with the oval in the first resist. She places it on the layers of fiber for the collar so that the 1" (2.5 cm) of fiber that overlapped the oval of the first resist extends through the hole. She presses the edges of these wisps of fiber over the edge of the second resist. With about one-third of the remaining fiber, she places 3 layers of wool over the wisps to build a frill smaller than the collar below, allowing 1" (2.5 cm) of the newly placed fiber to extend into the oval opening (Figure 3). When she is satisfied with the arrangement of the collar, she wets it with hot soapy water, covers it with the screen, and rubs with a plastic bag.

Figure 1. Sketch scarf on bubble wrap

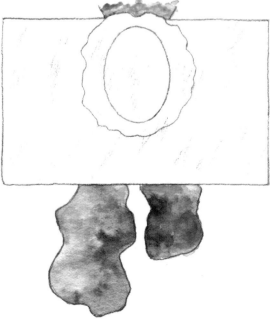

Figure 2. Sketch collar on plastic resist

Place resists and fiber for scarf ruffles

To create more ruffles on the scarf portion of the piece, Gar covers the wavy edges of the scarf with plastic resists (Figure 4). Repeating the process for the collar ruffle, she layers the remaining wool. The exposed portions are where the ruffles will adhere to the scarf. She repeats the wetting and rubbing process to attach this fiber at the center of the scarf shapes, producing an additional layer of ruffles.

Felt and full the entire piece

Removing the screen, Gar covers the piece with plastic sheeting and rubs it for 5 minutes on each side (being careful not to disturb the resists when she turns it over). She felts it using the rolling method. When the piece passes the pinch test, she puts it in the sink and beats it. (One alternative is to hurl it into the sink or slam it on the floor.)

Roll and stretch the ruffles

Once the piece is fulled, Gar focuses on the ruffles. She pulls and stretches the edges, applying heat if necessary, to thin and stretch them. Then she rolls the edges up and back between her fingers, repeatedly working the edges. If the ruffles are flat, she heats and stretches the base of the join to stiffen and support the ruffle.

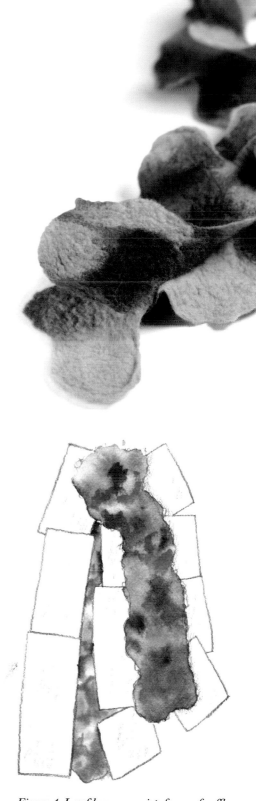

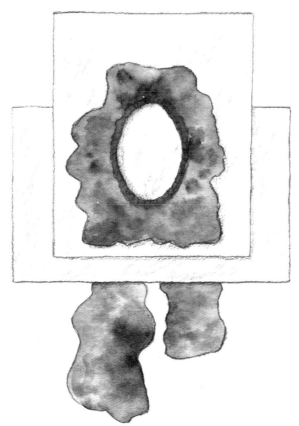

Figure 3. Layer fiber over second resist for collar ruffle

Figure 4. Lay fiber over resists for scarf ruffles

Heart Leaves

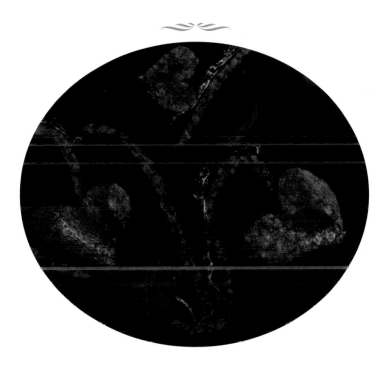

About the Artist

DIANA CLARK is known for her line of handbags and totes, which combine leather and alpaca felt. Her work can be seen at fine craft shows and on her website. She lives in Vermont.

Diana Clark's parents raise alpacas on their farm. Faced with an abundance of this lustrous and luxurious fleece, she found the perfect use in feltmaking. The natural colors of the fleece are the perfect foil for the brightly colored surface designs that distinguish her work.

The thick, soft, inviting chocolate-brown wall hanging pictured here can readily be replicated in merino wool roving by a handfelter. Thin strips of roving, designs cut from merino prefelts, and yards of eyelash or novelty yarns decorate its surface. Within the layers Diana has used a device employed in industrially produced felt: "scrim," a layer of open-weave fabric (in this case cheesecloth).

Key Techniques

- *Make prefelt in a pan*
- *Incorporate scrim*

Materials
- 1 oz (30 g) each of 7 colors of solid-colored merino for prefelts
- 2 oz (60 g) merino in accent colors for surface design
- 24 oz (720 g) solid-colored merino in main color
- 2 yd (183 cm) synthetic "fun fur" yarn
- 36 × 48" (91.5 × 122 cm) cheesecloth

In Diana's Studio
- 18 × 24" (45.5 × 61 cm) small bubble wrap
- 18 × 24" (45.5 × 61 cm) aluminum sheet pan
- Rolling pin
- 36 × 48" (91.5 × 122 cm) or larger bamboo shade, hardware removed
- 36 × 48" (91.5 × 122 cm) or larger nylon or polyester sheer curtain
- 36" (122 cm) pool noodle
- Metal watering can
- Kettle
- 3 ties made from pantyhose
- Ivory liquid soap
- Towels
- Scissors

Finished measurements
About 27 × 36" (68.5 × 91.5 cm); sample pictured measures 36 × 48" (91.5 × 122 cm).

Make and cut prefelts

Like many feltmakers, Diana likes to have several prefelts on hand to draw upon when creating her designs. She uses commercial sheet pans for simple and tidy prefelt making.

After lining the pan with bubble wrap with the bubble-side up, she builds 3 perpendicular layers of wool on it (Figure 1). She frequently makes bands of 2 or 3 colors per pan. Layering more than one color per band results in many shades and hues using few rovings. She strives for prefelts that are mottled and dappled, rather than one flat color.

When the layers are in place, she sprinkles them with Ivory liquid and boiling water from a metal watering can. She covers the fiber with the curtain and, using a rolling pin, flattens and presses the wet wool against the textured lining until it partially felts. When these prefelts, felted just enough to handle, are rinsed and dried, she cuts out shapes to use for surface design (here, about 40 hearts).

Create mat and place scrim

Diana divides the main color fiber into 6 portions. She covers a space 36 x 48" (91.5 x 122 cm) on the bamboo shade with wisps of fiber she pulls from one portion, arranging all the fibers horizontally. She crosses these with another portion of wisps arranged vertically and a third portion arranged horizontally. She covers the wool with cheesecloth before building 3 more layers.

Place surface design and felt the mat

Diana arranges the dry prefelt cutouts, remaining roving, and yarn as surface design. She sprinkles the wool with soap and hot water and covers it with the sheer curtain. She rolls the bamboo mat/wool/curtain layers up on the pool noodle to felt by rolling, then fulls it.

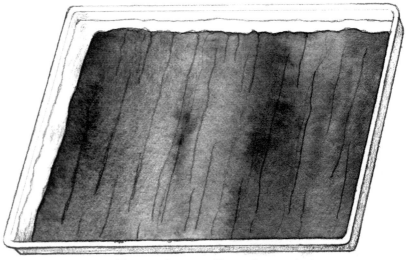

Figure 1. Create prefelt in a sheet pan

Fantasy Necklace

About the Artist
PHYLLIS DINTENFASS has lived
in the Midwest for nearly forty years.
Since retiring from a career in education,
she teaches beadweaving nationwide at
bead shows. She was twice juried into
the Bead Dreams competition at the
Bead & Button show. She lectures and
provides demonstrations on beadwork
with an emphasis on its historical and
ethnic significance. She shows her work
in galleries and select art shows. She
enjoys making her own felt beads for her
one-of-a-kind jewelry.

Phyllis Dintenfass credits her lifelong love of creating beaded
jewelry to growing up in New York City and living in Africa and
Europe, where she was exposed to a variety of cultures as well as
throngs of interestingly adorned people. As she can never have
enough beads, it was natural that making her own needle-felted
beads would appeal to her. Phyllis enjoys blending the colors and
sculpting the shapes of each felt bead; that a felt bead can be embellished with other beads compounds her joy. She likes to combine
her embellished felt beads with gemstones, pearls, metal, glass, and
bead-woven components.

Phyllis dreamed one night of some cloisonné-type beads in her
stash. They inspired a series of needle-felted beads that evoked
their design. Strung with filigree West African brass beads and
porcelain faux-cloisonné, she accentuated the felt beads while
balancing the design visually and physically.

Key Techniques

- *Needle-felt polyester*
- *Shape beads with needle felting*
- *Embellish felted beads
  with yarn and beads*
- *Plan, string, and crimp a
  felted bead necklace*

Materials
- 1.1 oz (30 g) polyester fiber-fill pillow stuffing
- .9 oz (25 g) Romney wool in accent colors
- 2 yd (1.8 m) Lurex yarn
- 7 g assorted seed beads
- Nylon beading thread
- Medium beading wire
- 2 crimp beads
- Assorted beads

In Phyllis's Studio
- Crimp tool
- 36-gauge felting needle
- Wooden handled 3-needle felting tool
- Scissors
- Serrated kitchen knife
- Beading needle
- Tapestry or doll needle
- Foam sponge needle felting surface

Finished measurements
Individual beads: 1¼" (3.2 cm) diameter round; 1½" (3.8 cm) diameter round; 1¾" (4.5 cm) diameter round; 2 cylindrical 1¼ × 1¼ × 2" (3.2 × 3.2 × 5 cm).
Completed necklace: 32" (81.5 cm) long.

Needle-felt round beads

Phyllis rolls a handful of polyester fiberfill into a tight wad. It is slippery and working against the foam sponge helps. She pokes directly into the center of the wad with the 3-needle tool, moving it up and down within the wad several times, pushing straight in and pulling straight out (Figure 1). Every few moments she rotates the wad and resumes poking. She makes 3 round beads that are similar in size though not identical.

Needle-felt cylinder beads

To make the cylinder beads, Phyllis works a double handful of polyfill fiber, rolling it along the sponge into as dense a tube as possible. She pokes along the length repeatedly, straight into the center and back up to the surface and moving the needle along ½" (1.3 cm) after every few pokes (Figure 2).

When entire length has been needled, she rotates the cylinder ½" (1.3 cm) away and resumes needling along its length. Phyllis works the entire cylinder this way until it is solid but soft. She cuts it in half with a serrated kitchen knife and continues to needle each piece until firm.

Cover beads with colored wool

Placing a few wisps of wool at a time, Phyllis covers the form of each bead with designs in colored wool (Figure 3). She pokes the 3-needle tool just below the surface of the wool in order to anchor the colored fiber without changing the shape of the bead. She may assemble flower shapes separately on the foam surface, needle them until they hold their shape, and attach them to the beads with more needle felting.

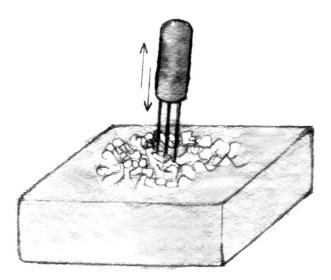

Figure 1. Needle-felt with tool

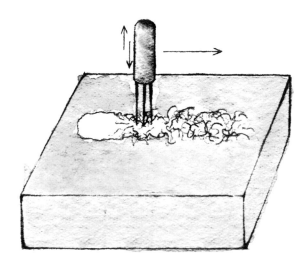

Figure 2. Needle-felt along cylinder

Outline decoration with Lurex

Phyllis prefers Lurex gold thread, a combination of polyester and viscose that is readily available. She uses a single felting needle to poke one end of the Lurex thread into the felt bead deeply to anchor it. Working a millimeter at a time, she slowly pokes the edges of the Lurex into the felt bead until each section is secure before proceeding with the next millimeter. She outlines the floral shapes to create the look of cloisonné (Figure 4).

Embroider the surface with beads

After anchoring the thread to the felt bead, Phyllis freely embellishes the surface with beads. With beading thread and a needle, she dots the surface with beads, placing one wherever the needle emerges from the felt and passing back into the felt where the bead has settled on the surface. She also employs bead embroidery stitches (such as backstitch, picot, and whipstitch).

Phyllis doesn't constrain herself to seed beads; she also likes the organic shape of tumbled gemstone chips. She adds them using a turning bead to prevent thread from showing on each side of the chip. She picks up a chip and a size 14° bead, then passes back down through the chip.

Figure 3. Decorate the beads with colored wool

Figure 4. Needle-felt Lurex thread to each bead

String the necklace

Phyllis designs her work from the bottom up without using the bead board that many stringers use. As beading wire alone is too soft to penetrate a felt bead, she places a tapestry needle on the end of the beading wire. If the beads are longer than the tapestry needle, she switches to a longer needle called a doll needle. She threads only 1" (2.5 cm) of the beading wire through the eye of the needle because it permanently kinks or creases the beading wire.

Centering the focal bead on the beading wire, she strings one side and then the other. Phyllis arrives at the final design through trial and error, expecting to restring before finalizing a design.

Finish the necklace

This necklace is meant to slip over the head, avoiding a clasp. When the beads are strung and she is content with the design, Phyllis is ready to attach the ends of the beading wire together using crimp beads and a crimp tool. She begins by cutting off the creased wire created by the needle. She picks up one crimp bead, another bead, and the second crimp bead. She crosses the other end of the beading wire through these 3 beads before crimping the crimp beads and trimming the ends of the beading wire.

Featherweight felt

Felt beads pose an interesting design challenge. An audaciously sized bead is nearly weightless, unless embellished with other beads. Though balanced visually, it may cause the necklace to be unbalanced physically, affecting the way it will be worn. Consider this when stringing each half of the necklace. Each bead's weight depends on the amount and type of embellishment.

Crimp beads and tools

Figure 5. Squeeze tool to crimp bead

Figure 6. Fold crimped bead into a cylinder

The crimp tool is a special pliers designed for the consistent, professional, and enduring crimping that is essential to quality beadwork. Inspect the crimp tool while squeezing it shut. Notice that there are two openings: the inside one resembles the silhouette of lips, the outer one the silhouette of an eye.

To use the crimp tool, allow the crimp bead to lie in the lower lip of the inner opening and adjust the two bead wires to lay parallel within the crimp bead. Squeeze the crimp tool. The center of the upper lip depresses or "crimps" the bead, securing the wires (Figure 5). Loosen your grip and slide the crimp into the outer chamber. Squeeze the pliers to fold the crimped bead in half, minimizing its appearance (Figure 6).

Circus Ottoman

About the Artist
NICOLE CHAZAUD TELAAR left the corporate world to form Festive Fibers, a full-time felt production and teaching studio. She and her husband, Tom Telaar, make beautiful, unique, and collectible objects for the home. Their work can be seen at museum and craft shows, gallery and museum exhibits, and their website, which posts their show and class schedule.

Nicole Chazaud Telaar was formerly a corporate textile designer, specializing in home furnishing fabrics. Since becoming a felt-maker, she enjoys this versatile, spontaneous and small-scale method of creating her own patterned fabrics. Nicole says she is passionate about all things wool: from the sheep that provide the fleece, to the fiber spun as yarn and woven or felted into fabric. Feltmaking brings together into one world many things she feels passionate about. She experiments lavishly with technique, color mixtures, and pattern layout, liberated by the knowledge that her investment of time, money, space, and materials is small. "Circus Ottoman" is the result of playing with laminated fabrics and unusual shaped trims in her line of felt upholstered furnishings.

Key Techniques

- *Prepare and pad a Sonotube for upholstering*
- *Paint and attach feet*
- *Sew the upholstery*
- *Upholster the ottoman*

Materials

- 13 oz (390 g) merino batt
- 14 oz (420 g) C1 Norwegian felting batt
- 18" (45.5 cm) square beaded sheer silk
- 44 loosely spun wool yarn strands, 18" (45.5 cm) each
- Sonotube core, 12" (30.5 cm) diameter, 11" (28 cm) inside diameter, $\frac{7}{16}$" (1.2 cm) thick, with end caps (see Sources, page 141)
- 14 × 14 × 2" (35.5 × 35.5 × 5 cm) upholstery foam
- 14 × 40 × ½" (35.5 × 101.5 × 1.3 cm) upholstery foam
- 4 decorative feet, 4" (10 cm) tall and 4" (10 cm) diameter
- Drywall screws
- Acrylic paint
- Spray polyurethane
- Gorilla glue
- Spray glue
- Lightweight upholsterers' staples

In Nicole's Studio

- 24 × 60" (61 × 152.5cm) solar pool cover or other felting mat
- 24 × 60" (61 × 152.5 cm) plastic sheet
- 24–36" (61–91.5 cm) pool noodle
- Dry cleaner or large can-liner bag
- Towels
- Dawn dishwashing liquid
- Watering can
- Vinegar
- 3 ties made from pantyhose legs
- Fine sandpaper
- Paint brush
- Bread knife
- Scissors
- Staple gun
- Screwdriver
- Straight pins
- 16" (40.5 cm) ruler
- 8" (20.5 cm) triangle
- Drill with variety of bits
- Sewing machine
- Spool and bobbin of thread

Finished measurements

18" (45.5 cm) tall; 12.5" (31.5 cm) diameter.

Pad the Sonotube and one end cap

A Sonotube is an extremely heavy-duty cardboard cylinder used for forming concrete footings. Nicole shares her source (see page 141) for those strong enough to be made into furniture using her method. Usually available without end caps, it is simpler and more efficient to purchase the Sonotube with those pieces already included, as from Nicole's source.

Nicole cuts the 2" (5 cm) thick foam to the exact size of the Sonotube end cap. (A bread knife works well.) She wraps the 14 x 40 x ½" (35.5 x 101.5 x 1.3 cm) upholstery foam around the Sonotube and trims if needed. Nicole squeezes small beads of Gorilla Glue around the inside lip of one cap (top). Gorilla Glue expands, so she uses it sparingly. Holding the cap on one end of the open Sonotube, she taps it with a rubber mallet if necessary to pop it into place. She sprays glue adhesive on the top of the endcap and places the round foam on the adhesive.

Next, she sprays glue on the Sonotube exterior and the edge of the 2" (5 cm) foam top to affix the ½" (1.3 cm) foam around the circumference of the Sonotube. She positions the edge of the ½" (1.3 cm) foam level with the top of the 2" foam, abutting (not overlapping) the ends. This join is where the side seam of the fabric will line up.

Paint and attach the feet

Ready-made but unfinished turned wood feet require some prep work before Nicole can paint them. Light sanding removes visible grain and nicks. She wipes off the wood dust before applying one coat of primer, 2 coats of paint, and 3 light coats of polyurethane.

Attach the feet

Nicole makes 4 equidistant marks 2" (5 cm) in from the edge of the second Sonotube end cap where the feet will be placed. She drills a hole to seat the screw. After attaching all 4 feet, she runs small beads of Gorilla Glue around this footed end cap and taps it into the bottom of the Sonotube. She lets all glue dry before covering the piece with the felt cover.

Make felt to upholster the ottoman

Nicole lays out fiber in the dimensions given below on her felting mat, overlapping strips of thin layers of wool batt or roving for each layer. (For production, Nicole uses a felting machine instead of the felting mat for the initial soft felting, then returns to felting and fulling by hand.)

Sides

To create a finished piece of felt that measures 15 x 42" (38 x 106.5 cm), and anticipating 25% shrinkage, Nicole arranges fiber over 54" (51 x 137 cm) of the felting mat.

Top

To create a 15–16" (38–40.5 cm) square, and anticipating 25% shrinkage, Nicole arranges fiber over a 20" (51 cm) square of beaded sheer silk fabric on the felting mat.

Flag trim

To create a 6 x 42" (15 x 106.5 cm) piece of felt, and anticipating 25% shrinkage, she arranges fiber over 8 x 56" (20.5 x 142 cm) of the felting mat.

Working in a spacious studio, with access to large mats and long rollers, Nicole simply rolls the work up lengthwise and felts it. When fulled to size, she rinses the felt and hangs it to dry.

Cut pieces for upholstery

When the felt is dry, Nicole presses it. She cuts the side piece to measure 15 x 42" (38 x 106.5 cm), the top to 14" (35.5 cm) round, adding ½" (1.3 cm) for seam allowance, and the flag strip to 6 x 42" (15 x 101.5 cm). She marks off every 3" (7.5 cm) of one long edge, creating 14 cells that will become 14 flags. Using a straight pin or tape, she marks a line 1" (2.5 cm) from the other long edge. This uncut edge will be the sewn-in edge. After marking the center of each 3" (7.5 cm) end of each cell (Figure 1), she cuts the line from there to the 1" (2.5 cm) line. Cutting along the lines, she removes one triangle as a template to perform the rest of the cuts.

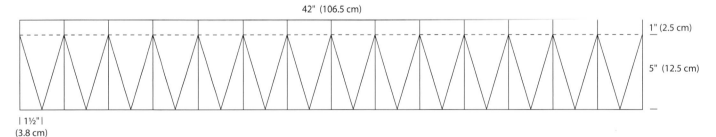

Figure 1. Flag trim

Sew the felt cover

With the 15 x 42" (38 x 106.5 cm) felt folded so that the right sides and the short edges are held together, Nicole sews the 15" (38 cm) edges with a ½" (1.3 cm) seam allowance, then trims the fabric close to the stitches.

Using straight pins, she pins the flag trim to the right side of the round fabric top, keeping the flags tucked to the inside while pinning around the circumference. She lines up the straight edge of the trim line with the outside edge of the top. Pinning the outside panel to the circumference of the top circle, she pins all 3 layers with right sides together and the flag trim in the middle.

She sews all 3 layers together, turns it right side out, and slips it over the foam-covered base to check for fit. Dropping a dry-cleaner bag or large can-liner over the ottoman helps the felt glide over the form.

Nicole wants the fabric to fit tightly. She makes seam allowance adjustments if necessary to keep the fabric taut. Once she is satisfied that it is snug, she trims all inside seams close to the stitch lines and turns the felt cover right-side out again.

Upholster the ottoman

Nicole slides the felt over the ottoman, rotating it so that the side seam falls over the foam-join line. Pulling tightly down towards the feet, she straightens the side seam and makes sure the circular top is even. Pulling it taut, Nicole staples the felt upholstery to the underside, about ½–¾" (1.3–2 cm) from the edge of the bottom.

Beginning by evenly centering each staple between adjacent feet, she places additional staples between each pair of staples. As the staples get closer together, she works the felt into small gathers, avoiding large overlapping pleats.

Making a second pass around, she places another round of staples about ¼" (6 mm) from the first.

The area around the outside front of the feet is a tight fit for the staple gun, so Nicole is careful not to scratch or nick the painted feet. When she has placed enough staples, she trims excess felt close to the staples.

A tight squeeze

Fitting the felt cover onto the ottoman will be a tight fit, a bit like zipping up too-small ski pants or putting on support pantyhose while still damp from the shower.

Carol Huber Cypher
Peacocky Scarf
37½ × 10" (95 × 25.5 cm)

Mindell Dubansky
Nasturtium Garland
70 × 3 × 3" (178 × 7.5 × 7.5 cm)

Bernard (Bernie) Bruce
Felted Chess Set
Board: 21 × 21" (53.5 × 53.5 cm)
Pieces: 2¾–6¼ × 1½ × 1½"
(7–16 × 3.8 × 3.8 cm)

Miriam Carter
Scarf
68 × 11" (173 × 28 cm)

Barbel Eggers
Floral Collar
30 × 5 × ½" (76 × 12.5 × 1.3 cm)

Kitty Moynihan
African Trade Bead Necklace
28½ × 1¼ × 1¼" (72.5 × 3.2 × 3.2 cm)

Phyllis Dintenfass
Beaded Felt Bead Pendant
6 × 1½ × 1½" (15 × 3.8 × 3.8 cm)

Theresa May O'Brien
Osman Carpet
35 × 41" (89 × 104 cm)

Carol Huber Cypher
Metamorphosis
6 × 2⅛ × 2⅛" (15 × 5.5 × 5.5 cm)

Gail Crosman Moore
Flower Lariat
48" (122 cm) long

Dawna Johnson
Sunlight Filtered Through Felt
40 × 29¼ × ¼" (101.5 × 74.5 × .6 cm)

Catherine Rogers
Jester Hat
23 × 6" (58 × 15 cm)

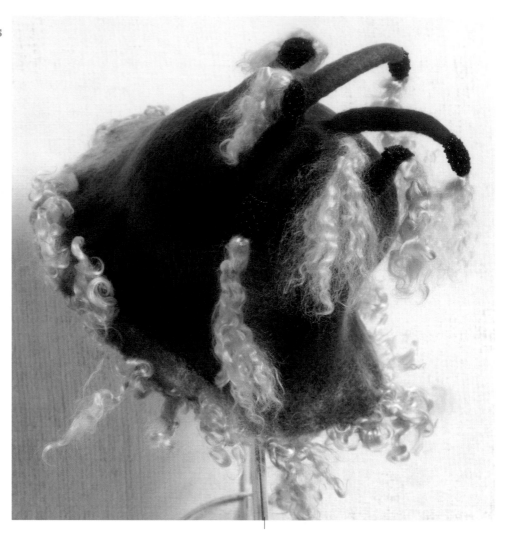

Lisa Klakulak
Purse
5 × 6 × 1¼" (12.5 × 15 × 3.8 cm)

Kitty Moynihan
Koi Pond
25 × 23 × 3" (63.5 × 58.5 × 7.5 cm)

Felting Basics and Information

The basic act of making felt involves applying pressure and agitation to wool in the presence of water and heat.

Ten steps to transform fiber into felt

1. Fluff

Open fiber by carding or striking with a bow (stick strung with a taut cord). The fiber used in these projects is readily available, fully processed, and ready to felt.

2. Crisscross layers of fiber

Arrange all the fiber, whether wisps of roving or strips from a batt, in one layer in one orientation. Top it with a layer of fiber perpendicular to the first layer. Continue in this way, alternating the direction of each layer, until the desired amount of fiber is placed.

3. Wet

Wet the wool with hot soapy water (unless otherwise specified). Water tends to bead on the surface of the fiber unless soap is added. The soap also acts as a lubricant. The fibers have more opportunity to tangle and knot when they move freely among each other. Each felter has her own preference; commonly used are olive oil soap in bar form, a slurry of grated bar and water, liquid castile soap, Joy or Dawn dish detergents, Ivory soap, and glycerine soap.

4. Cover

To protect the wet wool from shifting while it is rubbed, use plastic sheeting, can liner, drop cloth, or shower curtain; sheer curtains; fiberglass replacement window screening; mosquito netting; or pantyhose. (Some feltmakers find that soaping their hands liberally allows them to work without a barrier.)

5. Spread water throughout

Press pockets of air out of the fiber and distribute the water evenly.

6. Felt

Rub, tap, or roll the surface of the fiber until a skin forms. Roll the piece up in a felting mat made of bubble wrap; solar pool cover; a shade or beach blanket made from reed, rush, cane, bamboo, or matchstick; or, for smaller items, a sushi mat.

Some projects work best when the pieces and mats are rolled around a core such as a pool noodle or "fun noodle," foam pipe insulation, PVC pipe, a broomstick handle, or even a rolled-up towel. Tie the project and mat securely (but without knotting) using pantyhose legs, nylon straps, Velcro straps, or rubber bands. Roll the bundle back and forth gently to start, increasing pressure over time. Unroll the bundle, rotate the work, and resume rolling, working all 4 directions equally unless otherwise instructed. Many felters count 100 rolls back and forth and then change direction. The felt shrinks in the direction that it is worked. An alternative to rolling is to vibrate and press the fibers until they are felted. Apply the "pinch test" (see page 139) to determine if the fiber has felted. Determine the amount of shrinkage.

7. Full

To full the delicate fabric that has tangled and knotted enough to act as a surface and not individual fibers, use a textured surface such as a felting mat, washboard, stair tread, ridged door mat or boot tray, drain board, microwave bacon cooker, or car mat. Roll the felt across the textured surface with increasing pressure, simultaneously kneading and pressing it. Some feltmakers throw the piece forcefully against the sink or floor, while others make quick percussive strikes with a flat hand, paint stick, or ruler. Fulling compacts and condenses the fabric as it continues to knot and tangle. Alternating repeatedly between fulling and stretching heated felt hardens it. Expect the finished piece to shrink by 30 to 50%; the exact amount depends on amount and type of wool.

> ### Hairiness and shedding
>
> While fulling, the felt may start to shed. Place it in a plastic shopping bag and continue to work. This keeps it from pilling and encourages loose fiber to smooth back into the felt. Shave hairy felt with a disposable razor.

8. Rinse

Rinse under water to remove the soap. Many feltmakers add a splash of white vinegar to the rinse water, restoring the wool's pH. Some recipes specify water temperature while others call for alternating between extreme hot and cold.

9. Towel dry

Press the felt inside towels to absorb the water.

10. Shape

Block, pin, stretch, or press the felt until it takes on the desired shape, then allow it to air-dry.

Working with a resist

Resists are used to produce layers and three-dimensional effects in otherwise flat felt. To begin, cut a resist for the desired shape out of dense fabric, plastic, bubble wrap, vinyl, closed-cell foam, linoleum, or another material that the wool cannot penetrate. Onto the work surface covering, draw an outline of the resist and another outline 1½" (3.8 cm) larger than the resist. Wherever a seamless join is intended, the wool that is placed in the border area for the front will be smoothed around the edge to the backside. For flanges, wool placed in the border area for the front will be layered with wool placed there for the backside.

After felting the piece, remove the resist and commence fulling.

Have on Hand

Most of the items used in feltmaking are already at hand or easy to acquire. Though the recipes in this book express the individual feltmakers' preferences, there are many substitutes for nearly every essential.

Table

A collapsible banquet-size table of lightweight plastic is wonderful. Place each leg in a length of PVC pipe about 20" (51 cm) piece, depending on your height.

Towels

Cover the table with towels and have a couple extra on hand.

Water

Whether from a sink, a hose, a bucket, or some other device, access to water (and drainage) are essential. Depending on the technique, the water may need to be hot or cool.

Felting mat

Each piece in this book calls for a particular size. The largest size, 48 x 96" (122 x 244 cm), will work for any of them. Regular bubble wrap works well, and solar pool covers are an industrial strength version. Always choose small bubbles. Some pool supply stores sell pieces of solar pool cover as spa covers this size. Bamboo shades (with hardware removed) and grass beach mats, also work.

Roller

Pool noodles and pipe insulation are cheap, easy, and flexible. They provide a core around which to wrap the felting mat of choice.

Barrier

Choose crisp or high-density plastic over clingy plastic to hold wool in place as it is felting. Also keep a porous barrier that allows additions of water through it, such as mosquito netting, fiberglass replacement window screening, or curtain sheers.

Bubble wrap and solar pool cover make excellent felting mats. Sheer curtains keep wool in place while allowing water to pass through.

Foam pipe insulation (gray) and colorful foam "pool noodles" are useful cores for rolling around.

Ties

Cut the legs from 2 pairs of pantyhose. Use the top portion to fold the wool in place for hats and vessels. Reserve 3 legs for long ties and cut the fourth leg into 3" (7.5 cm) pieces, then slit the small rings open to produce several smaller ties.

Resist material

Closed-cell packing sheets, tiny-bubble bubble wrap, vinyl, and tight-weave fabric all make fine resists to prevent two layers of wool from felting together.

Textured surface

The classic surface is a washboard, but bubble wrap (bubble-side up), ridged mats, or stair treads also give excellent results.

Other supplies

Scissors

Ruler or tape measure

Permanent markers

Iron, steamer, or kettle

Sewing needle

Straight pins

Tape

Pantyhose are a multipurpose felting tool: The legs make great ties for rolling, and the top portions are used for making hats and vessels.

Fiber Preparations

Processed wool is available in many forms, from wide batts to pencil-thin roving. The main distinction in wool preparation is between carded and combed fiber. Though aligned somewhat by the carding process, carded fibers remain relatively random. Wool prepared on a barrel-shaped drum carder forms a **batt**; many batts blend beautiful colors and even different fibers. Strips pulled from the edge of a batt are called **sliver** (pronounced "SLY-ver"), while small clumps of wool prepared with handcards are referred to as **rolags**. Machine-carded wool is also available in long ropelike strips called **roving**; in common parlance most prepared wool is called by this name. By contrast, fiber made into **top** has been processed further by combing to remove the shorter, less desirable fibers and arrange them to lie parallel in a thick rope. Top tends to be more expensive than carded fiber, and because the fibers are so closely aligned it can be quite heavy.

Although both combed and carded fibers can felt readily, parallel fibers just glance off of each other. For them to mesh, knot, and tangle, they must cross each other, as in perpendicular layers. Carded roving is more random and will felt readily. Combed top can be pulled off in wisps that resemble brushstrokes.

Crisp or high-density plastic forms a barrier to keep wool in place while felting. Clear upholstery vinyl is an excellent resist material, keeping layers of wool from felting together.

Wool batt and pieces of sliver.

The weight of a wingspan

Grab the end of the Ashland Bay solid merino top with one hand. Unreel the roving from the wound ball by passing it through your other hand. Spread your hands as far as possible. This length of roving weighs about 1 oz (30 g)—not a precise measurement, but a good rule of thumb.

Combed fiber, like the merino top at left, is dense and ropelike. The carded Romney wool at right is looser and less perfectly aligned.

Handling Wool

Roving or top

Grasp the tip of one end of roving with one hand. Place your other hand around the roving about 8" (20.5 cm) away from the end. Pull gently and notice that wisps of fiber drift away from the roving. Notice the length of the fibers (staple length). Allow the distance between your hands to exceed the staple length when pulling off wisps of fiber, or you'll be tearing the fiber.

Batts

Prepare the wool by unfolding and opening the wool batt on a large table. Pinch the batt gently, as though opening a plastic bag, to separate long thin layers. Because clumpy batts are pesky, choose one that unrolls easily into long strips.

Types of wool

There are many breeds of sheep without even mentioning the cross varieties, and each has particular characteristics. Some wools require more time and effort to felt, and some don't felt well at all. All wool specified in these projects felts beautifully and is readily available. The following is an overview of these types of wool.

Merino creates a fine felt with a smooth finish, ideal for wearing next to the skin. The merino wool used in these recipes is specified as combed top or Australian carded batts.

C1 is a blend of wool from Norwegian breeds (Steigar, Rygia, and Dala) that felts beautifully. It is coarser and sturdier than merino, suitable for outerwear, shoes, rugs, and furniture. It blends with merino and is also appropriate for needle felting.

Romney is a great for needle felting, coarse enough to needle easily yet not itchy or hairy.

Glossary of common terms

Cuticle: The scales on the surface of each wool fiber that overlap like roof shingles. To experience this for yourself, hold a lock of your hair taut and pinch it loosely between the forefingers of your other hand. If you slide the pinching fingers from the tips to the roots, you'll notice a sticky feeling caused by the lifted cuticles resisting your fingers. If wool fibers are pressed and mingled while the cuticle is lifted, they catch and trap neighboring fibers as the cuticle closes, creating felt.

DFE: The abbreviation for "Directional Friction Effect," DFE is industry's term for the way wool fibers move. Influenced by their scaled surface (cuticle), taper, and length, the fibers are inclined to travel in one direction. Lubrication like water and soap, ease of movement by softening with heat, and applied pressure direct the individual fibers into endless circular movements that result in knotted and tangled fabric—felt.

Felt: Nonwoven material, two- and three-dimensional, produced by tangling wool.

Felt needles: 3-sided needles with barbs along the edges. Each poke of the needle drags the fibers in its path. Gauge (size) and barb placements vary. The artists here used 36-gauge for coarse fiber and 40-gauge for fabric and fine fiber. The "star" version offers more surface area and barbs for increased results per poke.

The barbs on felt needles cause the fibers to tangle and interlock. Needles can be used singly or in a holder.

Fulling: Shrinking and hardening of felt, making it stronger and firmer as the knots and tangles condense and become compacted under pressure and heat.

Habotoi: From the Japanese word for "soft as down," a smooth and evenly woven silk fabric. It is measured in *momme* (see below).

mm: Abbreviation for both a linear measurement (millimeter) and a measure of fabric weight (momme). Momme is a unit of weight for silk, pronounced to rhyme with "tummy." 1 momme = 3.62 grams per square yard. 5 mm is light and 10 mm is heavy.

Needle felting: Knotting and tangling fibers using barbed needles (see Felt Needles, above). Unlike traditional feltmaking, which relies on the cuticle structure of the wool, needle felting can be performed on fibers irrespective of their structure. Industrially produced synthetic/wool blends and even 100% synthetic felt—such as road subsurfaces, "pleather," filters, and acrylic craft felt yardage—are made by introducing fibers between opposing beds of felt needles that are moving toward and apart from each other. Barbs along the edges of the felt needles drag and tangle the fibers in their path with each poke.

Nuno: Also called laminated felt, a technique taught by Polly Stirling to felt thin applications of wool into delicate, open-weave fabrics, producing a supple and gossamer-like felt. Textured and colorful surface decoration can be applied to any open-weave fabric by felting wool into it; bits of nearly any fabric can be incorporated collage-style.

Pinch test: A method to evaluate that felting has occurred. When the pinched surface responds as one surface instead of as individual fibers, it is felted. Feltmakers learn to evaluate the degree of felting in this touch as a chef learns to check doneness in meat or fish.

Prefelts: Partially felted portions of wool that can be seamlessly joined to another piece early in the felting phase.

Scrim: Open-weave fabric sandwiched between wool layers in some industrially produced felt to reinforce it.

Sources

Aluminum sheet pan
Available in cooking supply stores.

Cotton thread
Metler mercerized cotton thread is available in sewing and craft stores.

Denatured alcohol
Available in hardware stores.

Drop cloth
Available in hardware or painting supply stores.

Dye (fiber-reactive)
PRO Chemical & Dye
PO Box 14
Somerset, MA 02726
(800) 228-9393
prochemical.com

Dharma Trading Company
604 Fourth St.
San Rafael, CA 94901
(800) 542-5227
dharmatrading.com

Felting needles
Available in craft stores and many yarn stores.

Magnets
(rare earth magnets, ½" [1.3 cm] diameter and ⅛" [3 mm] thick)
Amazing Magnets
amazingmagnets.com
(888) 727-3327

Mats (door, boot, car)
Available at hardware or home supply stores.

Mosquito netting
Available in camping or sporting goods stores.

Needle-felting mat
Foam sponge or upholstery foam appropriate for needle felting can be found in most craft stores.

Nonskid fabric coating
Performix Super Grip
caswellplating.com/aids/plastidip.html

Pipe insulation
Available in hardware and home supply stores.

Plastic sheet
Available in hardware, paint supply, and art supply stores.

Swimming or pool noodle
Available at pool supply and some children's toy stores.

PVC pipe
Available in hardware, home supply, and plumbing stores.

Shellac (blond shellac flakes)
Woodworkers Supply
1108 North Glen Rd.
Casper, WY 82601
woodworker.com
(800) 645-9292

Shoe lasts
(+45) 65 99 19 19 (Denmark)
kartehuset.com

Shoe soles
Sharon Raymond
Simple Shoemaking
145 Baker Rd.
Shutesbury, MA 01072
(413) 259-1748
simpleshoemaking.com

Silk
Chiffon and habotoi
Style Fabrics
(845) 338-1793
stylefabrics.com

Thai Silks
252 State St.
Los Altos, CA 94022
(650) 948-8611
thaisilks.com

Silk caps

Bonkers Handmade Originals
PO Box 442099
Lawrence, KS 66044
(785) 843-5875
bonkersfiber.com

Chasing Rainbows Dyeworks
Crown Mountain Farms, Dist.
(360) 894-1738
crownmountainfarms.com/html/
rainbows.html

Treenway Silks
501 Musgrave Rd.
Salt Spring Island, BC
Canada V8K 1V5
(888) 383-7455
treenwaysilks.com

Soap

Joy, Ivory, and other commercial dish
soaps are available at grocery stores.
Olive oil soap and Dr. Bronner's castile
soap are available in health food stores.

Solar pool cover

Available at pool supply stores.

Sonotubes
Furniture-grade Sonotubes

Seabury Distributors
16 Hillcrest Rd.
PO Box 97
Towaco, NJ 07082
(973) 335-8266

**Sonotubes of any size,
constructed with cap for top and
bottom**

Shapes Unlimited
(920) 788-5400 ext. 204
ron@shapesunlimited.com
shapesunlimited.com

Stair treads

Available in hardware and home supply
stores.

Waxed linen thread

Royalwood Ltd.
517 Woodville Rd.
Mansfield, OH 44907
(800) 526-1630
royalwoodltd.com

Wire

Available in hardware, craft, and elec-
trical supply stores.

Wool and mohair
Australian merino batts

Miriam Carter Merino
(603) 563-8046
miriamcarter.com

C1 Norwegian-blend felting batts

New England Felting Supply
feltingsupply.com

**Merino top (solid and multi-
colored); colonial wool top (solid
and multicolored)**

Amazing Threads
PO Box 758
Lake Katrine, NY 12449
(845) 336-5322
susan@amazingthreads.com
amazingthreads.com

The Wool Room
172 Joe's Hill Rd.
Brewster, NY 10509
(845) 279-7627
woolroom.com

For suppliers in your area, consult the
Ashland Bay Trading Company website
at ashlandbay.com.

Dyed Mohair locks

Stony Mountain Fibers
939 Hammocks Gap Rd.
Charlottesville, VA 22911
stonymountainfibers.com
(434) 295-2008

Dyed Romney wool

Black Sheep Designs
PO Box 56
Rensselaerville, NY 12147
(518) 797-5191
blacksheepdesigns.com

**Turkish merino and Turkish fattail
natural black wool**

woodscapeartistry.com

Artist Contact

Beth Beede
Northampton, MA

Linda Brooks Hirschman
lindabrookshirschman.com

Bernard (Bernie) Bruce
Mount Marion, NY

Elizabeth Buchtman
DesignsfromFenwood.com
Elizabeth@DesignsfromFenwood.com

Miriam Carter
(603) 563-8046
miriamcarter.com

Nicole Chazaud Telaar
Festive Fibers
PO Box 626
Alstead, NH 03602
(603) 835-2247
festivefibers.com

Diana Clark
alpacabagworks.com

Sharon Costello
blacksheepdesigns.com

Phyllis Dintenfass
Appleton, WI
phylart.com

Gail Crosman Moore
gailcrosmanmoore.com

Carol Huber Cypher
carolcypher.com
carol@carolcypher.com

Mindell Dubansky
New York, NY

Barbel Eggers
Stone Ridge, NY

Alexa Ginsburg
feltware.com

Omi Gray
(212) 864-4855
Omi519@aol.com

Dawna Johnson
dawna@athensculturalcenter.org

Heather Kerner
spiralworksfelt.com

Lisa Klakulak
strongfelt.com

Cassie Lewis
PO Box 185
New Milford, NY 10959
ccjj@warwick.net

Theresa May-O'Brien
woodscapeartistry.com

Jackie Mirabel
mirabelnaturals.com

Kitty Moynihan
Millerton, NY

Catherine Rogers
c.l.rogers@comcast.net
(978) 448-1273

Pat Spark
sparkfiberarts.com

Linda Van Alstyne
6339 Beizel Rd.
Middle Grove, NY 12850
northeastfeltmakersguild.com

Gar Wang
garron@warwick.net

Lucy Zercher
Chugiak, AK
(907) 688-5221

Index

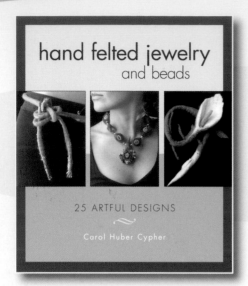

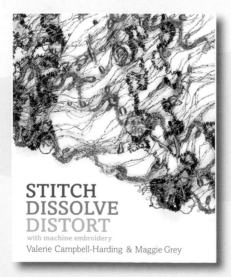